HYDROPONICS GARDENING

Learn the secret for growing plants in your garden with detailed hydroponics and aquaponics techniques. The ultimate guide for getting better vegetables and fruits

ANDREA M. WILSON

Copyright © 2020 by *Andrea M. Wilson*

- ALL RIGHTS RESERVED -

The content contained within this book may not be reproduced, duplicated or transmitted without direct written permission from the author or the publisher.

Under no circumstances will any blame or legal responsibility be held against the publisher, or author, for any damages, reparation, or monetary loss due to the information contained within this book. either directly or indirectly.

Legal notice:

This book is copyright protected. This book is only for personal use. You cannot amend, distribute, sell, use, quote or paraphrase any part, or the content within this book, without the consent of the author or publisher.

Disclaimer notice:

Please note the information contained within this document is for educational and entertainment purposes only. All effort has been executed to present accurate, up to date, and reliable, complete information. No warranties of any kind are declared or implied. readers acknowledge that the author is not engaging in the rendering of legal, financial, medical or professional advice. the content within this book has been derived from various sources. please consult a licensed professional before attempting any techniques outlined in this book.

By reading this document, the reader agrees that under no circumsta nces is the author responsible for any losses, direct or indirect, which are incurred as a result of the use of the information contained within this document, including, but not limited to, errors, omissions, or inaccuracies.

Table of Contents

Introduction..1

Chapter 1 What Is Hydroponic Gardening.........................5

   Why Plant Growth May Stop..9

   The Basics Of Hydroponics..11

Chapter 2 Managing Plant Health...................................15

Chapter 3 How to Build Your Own Hydroponic System............26

   Tools And All What You Need...27

Chapter 4 Best Plants for Hydroponics Gardening...................38

Chapter 5 Hydroponics Vs Soil Gardening and & Advantages and Disadvantages..45

   Hydroponics Vs Soil Gardening..45

   Advantages And Disadvantages.......................................47

Chapter 6 Myths and Mistakes to Avoid..........................53

   Myths...53

   Mistakes..57

Chapter 7 Growing Mediums & Nutrients and Lights................64

   Nutrient Solutions..64

   Growing Medium...65

   Light..69

Chapter 8 System Maintenance 71

Drippers 71

Ebb/Flood Systems 71

Ph 72

Supply Solution 72

Chapter 9 Problems With The Operation Of A Hydroponic System 81

Algae In Hydroponic 81

Possible Diseases And Pests In Indoor Plants 82

Healing Of Infested Plants 91

Chapter 10 Choosing Plants 93

Tomatoes 93

Blueberry 93

Strawberries 94

Watercress 94

Chives 94

Mint 95

Basil 95

Kale 95

Lettuce 96

Spinach 96

Radishes 96

Cucumbers *97*

Beans *97*

Peppers *97*

Peas *98*

Eggplant *98*

Cauliflower *98*

Cabbage *99*

Thyme *99*

Sage *100*

Rosemary *100*

Oregano *101*

Marjoram *101*

Lavender *101*

Fennel *102*

Dill *102*

Coriander / Cilantro *102*

Chervil *102*

Chamomile *103*

Catnip *103*

Anise *103*

Flowers *103*

Chapter 11 Tips and Tricks to Growing Healthy Herbs, Vegetables and Fruits **105**

Growing Plants On The Walls Of Moss *105*

The Basis *106*

Vertical Hydroponics *107*

Hydroponic "Life Hacks" *110*

Gardening Tricks *111*

Chapter 12 In Full Bloom: Secrets to Growing Hydroponics Herbs and Vegetables Successfully **114**

Plant Nutrients *114*

Ph TESTING *116*

Growing Healthy Herbs And Vegetables *118*

Cleanliness And Sanitation *119*

Pest Control *120*

Chapter 13 Light and Monitoring equipment **124**

Lights *124*

Monitoring Equipment *128*

Chapter 14 Hydroponics Media **138**

Media Originating From Rock Or Stone *139*

Medium Derived From Synthetic Materials *142*

Organic Media *142*

Conclusion **146**

Introduction

If you want to be successful in the hydroponic industry, then you only want skills, dedication, and must have a keen desire to grow crops. It is not necessary that the person who is going to do hydroponic gardening must have previous farming experience but it can be very helpful in understanding things in a better way.

With limited resources and surging population, traditional farming is on the back foot as there is a scarcity of land that's end number of growers are looking forward to hydroponic farming.

According to the latest report, it is stated that by 2050, there will be a drastic jump in the overall population that is from 7.3 to 9.8 billion. Due to this reason, there is a need for food which will surge from 58 % to 98% in the coming 30 years.

The farmers are concerned with regards to this as land is not available for the crops to grow. Thanks to hydroponic farming which has allowed growing the plants. The recent trend of hydroponic agriculture has captured the minds of farmers up to a great extent; that's why they are shifting from traditional farming to the hydroponic system.

The main benefits of this farming are it is very versatile; the system of hydroponic can be placed anywhere, etc.

Now, you will come to know the various mediums by which hydroponic system gets successful.

The system of hydroponic cannot compensate itself from poor growing conditions, lighting, water, pest issues, wrong fertilizers, etc. They need everything proper and in sufficient quantity so that that healthy plant will grow.

Well, let's start with some tips by which you can keep the garden on the non-stop path of success. Let's start with that: -

Light: The fruits and vegetables of hydroponic require an adequate amount of light, or you can say sunlight. According to the types of plants offer that light or sunlight accordingly so that they grow fast and yields better. Basically, the plants of the hydroponic garden need 8-10 hours regular sunlight each day for proper growth.

Room to grow: All plants need sufficient room to grow. The plants which rise above the ground require adequate space to live and expand and to carry out the work to make them eat. If they don't get sufficient room to grow, then it will impact the overall growth.

Temperature: There are many plants which like temperature as human-like. Some of the hydroponic plants need cold weather to grow, and some want hot for the best growth. So, make them feel comfortable like you feel relaxed at your dream house.

Water: The quality of water can be a very crucial issue in a hydroponic system. For the successful hydroponic gardening, you have to install reverse osmosis water and filter at the entry point so that the growth of the plants will be fast and yield a great result.

Oxygen: Hydroponic plants love to live insufficient air, and actually, they require a lot of it. They uptake oxygen to do their activities of absorbing water and nutrient uptake. However, the soil in which the plants are growing has a lot of oxygen, but the roots of the plants exhaust dissolved oxygen which can be dangerous for the plant. To be successful in oxygen supply, then adequate oxygen with the help of bubble air in the solution.

Hygiene: Whether it is a hydroponic plant or human being, hygiene is a must for both of them, which keeps them healthy and fresh. Always keep the surrounding area of the hydroponic system clean and tidy. When you are handling the plants, ensure that your plants are clean.

Nutrients: There are countless nutrients that are taken up by the plants in the water through roots. Fertilizers which are non-toxic help the soil to offer sufficient nutrient to the plants.

On the other hand, fertilizers are not the only thing which solves all your issues, but it also needs good light, soil, perfect drainage.

There are three major nutrients which are very essential for the plants that are nitrogen, phosphorus, and potassium. So, make sure that you will deliver these nutrients to the plants according to the quantity.

Time: Every plant needs time to grow, and for this, you have to care for them. There are many plants which take more time to grow, and some need less time. So, be patient while doing hydroponic gardening.

Support: In traditional farming, plants are supported by the soil for a strong foundation but, in hydroponic farming, the plants are offered artificial support in the form of netting or string type support which is one of the critical success in a hydroponic system.

Accuracy: When you are adding nutrients to the plants, make sure that you will use the EC meter or PPM so that it will be in precise quantity. This can be done with the help of the chart.

Well, these above tips are constructive for the growers if they want to get successful in the hydroponic system. Make sure that you take care of every small aspect of the hydroponic system.

Chapter 1

What is hydroponic gardening

To all flower lovers who are planning to grow plants without soil, Hans von Berlepsch's appeal to "first of all study the theory" in full so as not to remain handicraftsmen for the whole life fully applies. This is true: everyone can purchase a special hydro pot, plant a beautiful plant in it, and take care of it in accordance with the instructions. However, in this case, there is no understanding of the relationships and hidden processes. In order to know the life processes of a plant well, this is clearly not enough, and it is such knowledge that is of the greatest value to us.

How Hydroponic Gardening Works - Growing Plants In and Without Soil

The primary factor - the soil - has been closely associated with agricultural production since time immemorial. In the broadest circles, it has been taken for granted even today that humus-containing natural soil, with its infinite variety of small and tiny organisms, is an essential condition for normal plant growth. We affirm that we can do fine without soil, and we will try to substantiate this statement.

For someone who has a plot of land for growing plants, the expression "soil ripeness" should be well known. With the nutrient-rich, ripe soil, the highest yields are obtained. Let us try to examine the ripe soil and the "normal" soil more closely in general in order to determine the conditions under which the plants develop most luxuriantly.

We consider the soil, that is, the upper loose populated by plants, a weathered layer of the globe, as a three-phase system, characterized by always present three phases: solid, liquid, and gaseous. Any soil can serve as a habitat and a source of nutrition for plants only in the case of a favorable combination of these three phases.

In ripe soil, the ratio of these quantities, i.e., solid, liquid, and gaseous phases, corresponds to a proportion of 50:25:25. Half of the soil volume thus consists of a porous space, which again is half-filled with soil solution and a half with soil air.

Solid soil constituents are predominantly solid inorganic materials. They are a product of weathering rocks with sizes from large fragments to the smallest particles. The organic part of the solid phase of the soil consists of the decomposition products of animals and plant organisms and the metabolic products of animals and microorganisms.

Natural soil is characterized by an endless variety of microorganisms that feed on the organic part of the soil. During this process, organic matter is completely decomposed to form water and carbon dioxide, and the mineral food products of plants contained in the organic mass are converted into a form in which they can be absorbed by plants. Along the way, microorganisms due to complex chemical and biological processes contribute to the further weathering of inorganic particles, and new quantities of plant nutrients are released.

Thus, we can state that the totality of organisms living in the soil fulfills an extremely important task in it - in combination with other factors (various weathering factors), continuously replenish the sources of nutrients in the soil.

During the so-called mineralization process just described, plant nutrients such as nitric, phosphoric and sulfuric acids, etc., are formed, which form salts with calcium, potassium, magnesium, etc.

The formation or release of vital trace elements (boron, copper, manganese, etc.) occurs in exactly the same way. All these chemical compounds important for plant nutrition can be absorbed by them only with water, which serves as a means of dissolution and movement. Thus, soil moisture is a nutrient solution containing substances that are essential for plant nutrition. It must again be emphasized that the source of plant nutrition is only the soil solution with the nutrients it contains. On the contrary, organic compounds can be considered as sources of nutrients only after their complete microbiological decomposition. (Organic matter, of which the dry matter of plants is about 95%, is formed by the plant itself from water and carbon dioxide with the help of solar energy. They are never extracted from the soil in the finished form. The soil only supplies the missing 5% of mineral compounds).

It should not be forgotten that water is necessary not only as a solvent and a vehicle, it also serves as a nutrient in the construction of plants and, in addition, performs other various psychophysiological tasks (for example, promotes the swelling of colloids, etc.) No plant is not able to grow without water, and in general, life without it is impossible. Lack of soil moisture can greatly reduce yield.

Now about the soil air. It should, apparently, play a rather large role, because we always strive to promote its aeration by cultivating the soil. This is understandable given that every living thing breathes, and therefore, requires oxygen. This, of course, applies not only to plant roots and storage organs (tubers, bulbs, etc.) but also to other organisms in the soil. If the surface of the soil coalesces so that normal air exchange is hampered, or if excess water in the soil displaces the soil air, then the underground parts of the plants suffer from a lack of oxygen. In this case, animal organisms inhabiting the soil can compete with cultivated plants with respect to oxygen consumption. Therefore, we must always take care of it.

We discussed very briefly how ripe soil should look, in which plants, apparently, should develop in the best way, or what fertile soil should be. From the foregoing, we can conclude about the conditions necessary for growing full-fledged plants also without soil.

First of all, each plant requires a habitat in which it can be fixed by roots. And here it does not matter at all whether the roots will be in the mass of rice husks, gravel, peat chips, or coal slag. The substrate performs only a physical role and has nothing to do with plant nutrition. For this, a so-called nutrient solution is used.

A nutrient solution, as a natural source of plant nutrition, should contain all the compounds that a plant needs for lush growth and fruiting in the right form, sufficient concentration, and in proper proportions. Countless experiments with nutrient solutions have made it possible to clarify the needs of well-known cultivated plants so well that we can now make recipes for nutrient solutions. Periodic resumption of the solution and its regular monitoring and replenishment of the loss of individual components allows us to provide good nutrition to our pets.

Microorganisms inhabiting natural soil are completely redundant when growing plants without soil due to the use of a ready-made nutrient solution. From it, plants receive all the food in an already digestible form, and there is no need for its processing. The nature of this or that artificial substrate does not need any influence from soil microorganisms. (In natural soil, we are very grateful to the organisms living in the soil for the formation of so-called soil aggregates.) Thus, we can choose materials that, after appropriate preliminary processing, will correspond in their structure to the structure of ripe soil (50% solid particles, 50% porous space). By this, we already provide a fairly good supply of oxygen to the root growth zone, and thanks to the method of supplying the nutrient solution — and we will learn more about this below — we can achieve a really optimal supply of air.

Summarizing the above, we state that plants can be grown without any soil. You only need to be able to observe and simulate the processes occurring in the soil. If we can provide our pets with everything that is in fertile soil, then we will achieve the same goal - the lush growth of healthy plants.

Why plant growth may stop

If this happens, then you should immediately remember the "law of the minimum." What is meant by this?

Let us allow ourselves a little digression and imagine the walk of a family with small and older children. The family moves quite slowly forward, because the short legs of the children, perforce, determine the pace of movement. A little imagination, and we will be able to formulate a law: the speed of the family is limited by the feet of the youngest child - it is a limiting factor!

In the development of plants, similar circumstances play a role. The development of a plant is determined not by the growth factors available in the optimal amount, but by those that are lacking, which, therefore, are at a minimum. For this reason, even the best fertilizers and irrigation will not give anything if you try to grow some light-loving plant in the dark...

The fact that there is not enough growth factor that determines the boundaries of a plant's development even when there are optimal quantities of other factors is called the "Law of the Minimum".

One clever and humorous gardener taught his students to always remember the five letters if they want the plants to grow. He had in mind the capital letters of the names of factors that are crucial for plant growth: light, water, air, heat, and nutrition. If a plant is provided with all these factors, it can fully manifest itself; that is, its growth will be most magnificent.

Using the method of growing plants without soil, we can directly affect the supply of plants with water, nutrition and, with a known skill, bring it closer to optimal. However, we should never forget about other factors - light, warm air, and, as far as possible, we will take into account the special needs of individual decorative and healthy plants. These factors should not be limiting. There is a lot of good literature available for a more detailed look at these issues.

The basics of hydroponics

What do your plants require?

Both plants need the right conditions to reach their full potential. Plants grown by systems of hydroponics are no exception to this fundamental rule. As their soil relatives, they require adequate light of the appropriate wavelengths, an adequate temperature, adequate supply of water, enough oxygen, mineral nutrients and structural support.

An adequate light of the right wavelengths is important for the plant's survival at its growth stage. Plants use a lot of light every day, at least 8 to 12 hours, to generate carbon dioxide and water. The green color of plants, chlorophyll, absorbs the sunlight and uses its energy to synthesize these carbs.

This process is called photosynthesis and is the basis for the survival of life in all plants. As animals and people eat plants, it can also be viewed as the source of our lives. Artificial lighting is generally a poor substitute for sunlight as most indoor lights do not produce a mature crop in sufficient intensity.

High intensity lamps such as sodium high-pressure lamps will supply over 1000 foot light candles. The hydroponic gardener can very effectively use these lamps in areas where sunlight is not adequate.

Nevertheless, the machinery and lamps are typically too costly for a small commercial company to operate. It is essential that there is ample spacing between plants, as this ensures that every plant gets enough light in the growing room.

For example, plants of tomatoes cut into one stalk must be planted to give 4 square feet per plant, while seedless cucumbers of 7 to 9 square feet and seeded cucumbers of approximately 8 square feet must be permitted in Europe.

The salad plants must be 7 to 9 centimeters apart in row and 9 centimeters between rows. Most other vegetables and flowers should be planted at the same distance as for the traditional greenhouse.

For the plant to grow normally, a suitable temperature is needed. Too high or too low temperatures can cause an irregular development and decreased performance. Summer and most flowers are best grown between 60 ° and 80 ° F, while winter vegetables such as spinach and lettuce tend to have temperatures between 50 ° and 70 ° F.

Appropriate water is usually not a concern in the use of a hydroponic system, since water containing solution nutrients is the basis of hydroponics. However, there are some systems that can cause insufficient watering, with the resulting adverse results for your plants.

Ebb and flow systems not tested on an appropriate basis can run short of nutrients, as can continuous flow systems in their storage tanks. Most, if not all, automated hydroponic systems can have catastrophes unless closely monitored.

Blocked or burst pipes or pump failure can lead to a lack of nutrient flow, resulting in dry roots and severe damages to or even deaths of your plants together with extreme lighting and the appropriate ambient temperature in the growing room.

Oxygen is a fundamental requirement for most living things. Plants require breathing oxygen to take water and nutrients. There is normally enough oxygen in soil environments, but plant roots in water use the supply of dissolved oxygen quickly.

This may harm or even destroy the plant without the provision of additional air. The bubbling air through the solution is a common way of ventilating the nutrient. Continuous flow and aeroponic systems typically do not require additional oxygen.

Many green plants require mineral nutrients. To order to survive, they must consume certain minerals from their roots. Such minerals are provided by the soil and the application of fertilizers such as manure and compost in modern horticulture.

The large quantities of nitrogen, phosphorus, potassium, calcium, magnesium and sulfur are required and only very small quantities of nitrates, iron, manganese, zinc, copper, molybdenum and chlorine are needed.

The soil surrounding the growing plant normally provides support. Nevertheless, a plant grown with hydroponics must be artificially assisted. Typically this is achieved by string or stakes. You can buy cheap automatic string rollers to help your plants as they grow. This reduces the tedious task of continuing to adjust strings in rapidly growing plants.

Chapter 2

Managing plant health

Diagnosis:

Problems fall into three possible classifications:

1. Nutritional–there is either too little or too much of one or more specific nutrients.

2. Environmental-Conditions for the environment are not ideal.

3. Pathological-One or more organisms tamper with the plant's health. Such organisms are called pathogenic agents. To be able to diagnose plant diseases, it requires a lot of knowledge and expertise. Do not expect such an ability to develop quickly. The first and perhaps most important skill to develop is the ability to inspect a plant and look for the telltale symptoms that can be indicative of what may be wrong.

Telltale symptoms

1.   Wiltingdue to insufficient soil water.

Leaves dry out quicker than the rate at which water is taken up by the root (the weather is too hot).

Something stops water from getting up the stem, e.g. borer, disease, etc. in the lower part of the plant. It is best to watch the plant closely.

Yellow leaves

In older leaves, if there is:

Nitrogen shortage (nitrogen fertilizer should be used)

Nitrogen shortage caused by wet soil—wet soil stops nitrogen from being taken into the plant (improves drainage or reduces watering).

Chemical damage.

Very dry soil.

If it is in younger leaves:

Iron Deficiency.

Deficiency in other nutrients.

Also causes chemical damage.

Measurement of damage

Look to see if the damage is uniformly distributed over the plant.

Check for the pattern: Only on one side?

Only at the top?

Is one of the parts more exposed?

Duration of damage

See if the damage has just occurred or has occurred in the past.

The appearance of the growing tips helps you decide the current state of the plant.

Young shoots imply a healthy plant that is overcoming past issues.

Excessive side shoots that are lower down indicate hormone flow disruption in the plant.

Physiological problems

There are several environmental factors, which, unless properly controlled, can lead to the damage of a crop. Frost or extreme supply of sunlight may burn fruit or leaves, and fruit may break, and leaves may discolor. Some of the commonest issues are detailed below.

Cracking: Lack of water or excess water may cause a split in the skin of different crops. Occasionally, newly picked carrots split up. Tomatoes that suffer from water shortage and that are exposed to high temperatures may split.

Blossom root rot: A common tomato problem is where the tomato bottom appears to be brown or black and leathery. It usually happens when there is a low calcium supply combined with erratic development, which causes stress in the plant. This problem is also associated with irregular and variable water supply and varying temperature conditions.

Crooking: This is where the fruit is warped (for example, cucumbers tend to be excessively curved). Crooking has been directly linked to poor temperature, humidity or nutrition control.

Common diseases and their control in hydroponics

Alternaria

This blight normally affects leaves and occasionally stems. Symptoms are typically spots and often develop clustered circles as they grow. There are several varieties of alternarias. Most of them are regulated by Zineb. A spray of copper will regulate some of these.

Anthracnose

Two different groups of anthracnose infections, which can be classified by their symptoms are:

1. Dead spots are a common symptom.

2. Symptoms include abnormal growth of some parts of the plant (e.g. an elevated boundary around a depressed central area of undeveloped tissues). Different fungicides can manage anthracnose. Copper sprays control some varieties, others by Zineb and other chemicals.

Botrytis

A gray fuzzy moldy proliferation that develops on roots, branches, fruits and berries, botrytis occurs in damp, rainy conditions.It is necessary to remove affected parts and burn them instantly. Preventive measures include increased airflow and decreased moisture. It is possible to use thiram and dichlofluanid fungicides to control these infections.

Downy mildew

A plant's upper leaf with this disease shows yellow discoloration or dull splotches sprouting underneath with a gray mold. It occurs under most circumstances and is regulated by Zineb.

Fusarium

Symptoms may include yellowing of the leaves, stunted growth, wilting and dropping of leaves. Commonly, proper sanitation should regulate fusarium.

Phytophthora

There are several modes of Phytophthora ranging from the disease of new seedlings stem to other forms that affect nutrient uptake in very large plants. Symptoms are often drastic and can cause the plant to suddenly die. Remove contaminated sections and clean affected areas. Fongarid will control some modes of phytophthora effectively, and reduce the spread of others.

Powdery Mildew

The disease occurs in dry, tropical, humid conditions. A chalky white growth on leaf surfaces is the principal symptom. Sulfur sprays or dust would usually provide regulation.

Water Management

Water Requirements

Plants in their habitat need both water and oxygen. Sometimes, the trick to successfully grow plants is to provide the right delicate balance between those two. Typically too much air means too little water, and usually, too much water means insufficient air. Throughout aggregate culture, a well-drying medium (e.g. gravel) will typically be combined with a moisture-retaining medium (e.g. vermiculite) to achieve the necessary water retention balance.

Water accounts for 90 percent of the total weight in many fruits; water content of leaves is 80 percent and that of seeds is 10 percent. In addition to its function in the plant parts, composition water is also essential for the movement of nutrients into the plant and waste products out. In a plant, everything migrates in a dissolved state. If water is not replaced constantly the cells lose turgidity and the plant wilts.

Excess Water

Symptoms of excessive water are:

• Development of long, slender seedlings. This usually occurs when the plants become too close together and the soil, as in glasshouses, is warm and humid.

• Presence of growth cracks (in fruits of tomatoes and heads of cabbages or carrots).

• Increased size of cells.

• Lengthy internodes (longer distances between buds and stems).

• Cells bursting (when viewed under a magnifying glass). Typically this is due to poor irrigation or overwatering. Excess water can cause stunting, diebacks appearing on top of the plant and, in extreme cases, can lead to death. In a wet situation, there is a greater probability of infection with rots, molds, and other fungal diseases.

Symptoms of water deficiency:

- The first and more common symptom is that the growth rate will gradually start to decline.

- Leaves gradually shrink (although no sign of discoloration).

- Later the branches get shorter, and the flowers and fruits become smaller.

- The plant also draws water from half-grown fruits from some watery fruits (e.g. strawberries, lemons, cherries, etc.) allowing the fruit to wither away.

- Appearances of diebacks from the leading shoots can happen, leading to death in extreme situations.

- A case of water shortage may be due to underwatering; poor root system; excessive drainage; or sometimes intense heat (i.e., water is sometimes dried up from the leaves faster than it can be absorbed by the roots in hot and windy conditions).

Water relationships

Before constructing an irrigation system, an understanding of the relationship between the root environments, plants, and water is required. The root environment consists either of a solid substance consisting of particles of different sizes and shapes that mesh together imperfectly to form a dynamic system of pores and channels or an enclosed environment filled with water in either a gaseous or liquid state (or both for NFT).

With a solid material, the medium gets saturated as pore spaces are filled with water. This can happen after irrigation or rainfall. A medium will only stay saturated when there is no unrestricted draining of excess water. The amount of water that a medium can hold at saturation is dependent on the volume of available pore space. That is known as the capacity to saturate.

Moisture can be divided into three types within a stable medium:

1. Gravity water–This water can only last for a short time in the medium before it flows under gravitational force.

2. Capillary water–This is the primary source of water for plant growth, appearing on solid particles as a thin film or as particles in the pore space. The surface tension holds it up in place. (When gravity has drained all the free water, an equilibrium is achieved where the surface tension binds all the remaining water so that gravity is unable to expel it. This condition is called field capacity).

3. Hygroscopic water–This is a thin film of water so firmly held to the solid particles that it cannot be absorbed by the plants. Through a process called transpiration, plants use water. The plant acts as a pump, drawing water (against the forces which hold it in the medium) into the roots of the plant, stems, and leaves from where it is lost through evaporation to the atmosphere.

Evaporation happens as water is drawn into the air and temperature, humidity and wind are determined by climatic characteristics.

If the temperatures and the rate of evaporation are high, a plant will need more water from the medium than when it is low. Plants are ready to use free water; however, there is a need for increased suction to remove surface tension holding water.

When plants reach a stage where they can no longer draw sufficient water to meet their needs, they may start dropping. This is also the Wilting Point. If at this stage water becomes available, the plant will recover; however, if it continues without water, it will reach a point where it is beyond recuperation.

This is regarded as the persistent point of wilting. The difference between the permanent wilting point and the moisture content of the soil is known as the water available. The amount of water retained, and the amount tightly bound, can vary from medium to medium.

When to irrigate

The region between the wilting point and the field potential is critical in irrigation, intending to preserve the level of moisture within this zone. It has usually been observed that plants take most of their needs from the upper half of the root zone and thus only about half of the available water is expended.

Therefore, irrigation is generally required when roughly half of the water available is used up. Hence, when the medium is at field capacity, the amount of water to be applied to a crop is half the water available in the root zone of the plant. The timing of irrigation applications depends on how fast the plants use the available moisture and this is usually dependent on climatic conditions and nutrient availability.

Also important is the rate at which water is supplied through irrigation, and it is governed by medium rates of infiltration, i.e. the rate at which water passes into the medium. If it can be absorbed by the medium at a rate lower than the water is supplied, runoff may occur, and water may be wasted. The ideal situation is where the rate of application equals the rate of infiltration.

Plants greatly require water to grow and survive. Nonetheless, the amount of water needed can differ from one plant to another. The two principal factors affecting how much water a plant needs to survive are:

1. Plant Variety

Some certain plant types have the ability to retain water for subsequent use within their tissues. This is not possible with other plants

2. The setting in which the plant grows

When there is plenty of water available around the plant it prefers to remain moister than in open, windy, warm conditions. A plant may suffer from water shortage but it may also suffer from an unnecessary increasein the supply of water. It is important, when watering a plant, to strike that delicate balance between too little and too much. Overwatering can be as severe as underwatering.

Chapter 3

----- ❧☙ -----

How to build your own hydroponic system

First, line your Styrofoam box with the black bag and then fill it with distilled water.

With your cups, trace six circles on the lid cover (the deep part) that are evenly spaced. Using a knife, cut out circles that are a quarter inch smaller than the traces.

Cut a small hole in the bottom of each of the Styrofoam cups and fill it with moss and perlite (only up to under the cup's rim).

Sow lettuce seedlings in the perlite and fill in.

Water the seedlings every day with the nutrient mix. You can do this at the same time each day so you will not forget. Always check that the water level in the container is not too high.

After 7 to 10 days, you will see roots spring out from the seedlings and they will enter the container.

As the lettuce matures, harvest them as you need them. Remember not to over harvest or the plant will die.

When you are successful with this first hydroponic garden, you can move on to try other plants and other systems.

Setting up the hydro unit is also easy and you can purchase the nutrient mix from gardening stores. One of the tricky parts is how to germinate hydroponic seeds and how to transplant them in the hydro units and your own little hydroponic garden is ready.

Tools and all what you need

As you venture into hydroponics farming, there are specific tools you need to get you started. Although there are several systems from which you shall choose, the kind of tools used in all of them is more or less the same.

The tools you will need include:

A reservoir

From its name, the reservoir will be used for reserving the nutrient concentrate. The concentrate is typically a mixture of water and the required plant nutrients and depending on the kind of hydroponic system you choose to install; the liquid is pumped from it periodically into the growing chamber as set at the timers.

In some systems, the reservoir doubles as the growing chamber too, such that the plants grow suspending their roots in the nutrients concentrate 24 hours, every day.

You do not have to purchase a special reservoir; you can fashion it from almost any inert large container that you use to hold water, so long as it does not leak. The container should be able to hold enough of the solution to allow it to grow. In addition, the container should be opaque to prevent the rays of the sun from penetrating into the solution.

If the container available to you is not opaque, there are many ways to make it light proof. For example, you could wrap or cover it up with an opaque material, or you could paint over it. The idea behind the opaqueness is to prevent algae from growing on the inside of the container.

If the hustle of making your own reservoir seems a bit too much, you could also opt to purchase the commercial reservoirs, and they will serve you well.

A growing chamber

A growing chamber is one of the most critical parts of a hydroponic system because this is where the plant roots develop. The chamber is the container that holds the roots, provides support to the entire plant, and house the nutrient concentrate.

The chamber, just like the reservoir, should be kept from direct sunlight and extreme temperatures because these can introduce heat stress to the plants. In case of exposure to extreme temperatures, such as heat, the plants abort their fruits and flowers.

The size and shape of the growing chamber are dependent on the kind of hydroponic system you intend to run, and the plants you wish to grow. Plants that grow big roots will require a large growing chamber while those that develop small roots will be okay with just a small one. However, do not be stressed about sizes because any chamber size will make due so long as the plants you are growing get their deserved nutrients and space.

In your quest to find the best growing chamber, kindly keep off metallic containers because metals are subject to corrosion and they react with the nutrient concentrate. If you cannot purchase a commercial growing chamber, however, check around to see the non-metallic items you could transform into growing chambers. However, if you still need to maintain class and style while at it, you could opt for a commercial growing chamber; there are some fabulous makes available, and I am certain they will appeal to your pallet.

Delivery system

The delivery system is the system that delivers nutrients to the plant roots directly. The concept of this is quite simple, in fact, and can be customized to fit into any system you choose to take up and install. A typical delivery system must include connectors, PVC tubes, blue or black vinyl tubing, and tubing connectors, for garden irrigation.

Depending on the hydroponic system that you settle for, you can choose to use emitters and sprayers for the delivery system. Although the sprayers and emitters are quite useful, be prepared, however, for frequent clogs when the nutrients in the solution build up. Therefore, if you are looking forward to stress-free farming, avoid them as best as you can.

Submersible pump

Most pumping systems have a submersible pump to regulate the pumping of the nutrient concentrate from the reservoir to the growing chamber. You can buy these pumps at home improvement stores or hydroponic shops in your area. The pumps come in varying sizes, and you just have to choose one that matches the size of your farm.

How do submersible pumps work, you ask? Well, the pumps are just impellers that take advantage of electromagnetic fields to spin then pump their water. It is easy to maintain them because the majority of the time, you are only required to clean the solution filter. If you bought your submersible pump without a filter, you could still make one by cutting some part of the furnace filter, ensuring that it fits the submersible pump.

Besides the filter, you also need to clean the pump occasionally to ensure that there are no clogs that would obstruct the nutrients as they flow to the plants.

Air pump

Although it is not compulsory that you make an air pump part of your hydroponic system, you ought to give it a thought because it comes with so many benefits. An air pump is also widely available in stores, and inexpensive, particularly if you are able to buy yours at a store that sells aquarium supplies.

An air pump is primarily used to ensure that there is a steady supply of oxygen in the water so that the roots can absorb it for their respiration, in the growing chamber. The pump does this by pumping the air through the airlines, onto the air stones, which ten creates bubbles that bubble up into the nutrient solution.

In case you are using a water culture hydroponic system, for example, the air pump keeps the roots from drowning in the nutrient solution because they are kept suspended in it all day, every day. In other hydroponic systems, the air pumps are fitted into the reservoirs to keep pumping oxygen into the water, increasing the oxygen concentration in the water.

Since the air pumps pump all day, they cause constant movement, which keeps the water and nutrients in it in constant motion. The circulation that results from the process ensures that the nutrients dissolve into the water evenly, at all times. The presence of oxygen in the water is also good because it prevents the growth of pathogens and microbes.

Timer

Not all hydroponics farmers need to time their operations with a timer, based on their choice of hydroponics system and its location. If your system is to be situated indoors, for example, and you have installed artificial lighting, you need to install a timer that will turn the lights off or on.

Drip and aeroponics systems also need a timer to control their submersible pump that controls the process of draining and flooding. It is important to take note of the fact that some types of aeroponics would need some special kind of timer to work properly.

Although the light and standard pump timers work very well, it is better to opt for a timer that has a 15 amperes rating other than 10 amperes rating because the former is often heavy duty and will have a cover that effectively protects it from water.

You only have to check at the back of the packaging of the timer you choose to ensure that you have made a good choice.

But for those who may have a battery backup, a digital timer is not preferred over an analog one because once you unplug it from the power source, it loses all the data previously stored in it. Analog timers are a better choice for the additional benefit of having on and off settings. Therefore, as you go out to purchase a timer, ensure that yours has pins all around the dial, so that you get the analog kind, and avoid future regrets.

Growing medium

The growing medium is essentially the substance on which the plants grow. It provides physical support to the plants, just like soil does, only that it is inert, not containing any minerals or living organisms. Different systems demand different growing mediums. For example, while other systems use peat moss, Rockwool or lava stone as the growing medium, aeroponics system uses air as the growing medium.

Nevertheless, the right kind of medium is one that retains moisture in such a way that the water solution will not need to be pumped in continually, every single minute.

Growing lights

Grow lights: you can have them you can stay without them. They are an optional part of the system because it all depends on where you intend to plant your garden. You may end up using natural light or having to take up artificial lighting for your plants. If possible, opt for natural lighting because it is free, and will not add to the cost of setup as you purchase the new equipment and its accompanying maintenance costs.

If, however, you cannot find any good lighting at the place you intend to plant your garden by having lots of exposure through the window or having a sunroom, or that the time of the year does not allow enough lighting through, you may need to include some supplemental artificial lighting in your set up budget.

Kindly realize that your ordinary bulbs cannot be used as grow lights: grow lights are specially made light bulbs that emit light containing special color spectrums that mimic natural light. Your plants will take in these color spectrums and use them to carry on the process of photosynthesis, hence the leaf growth, flower formation, and fruit growth. Realize also that the intensity and type of light that the plant has access to, by large, determines its photosynthetic abilities.

Most hydroponic kit systems will come with complimentary light fixtures, but if you are setting up a DIY (Do It Yourself) garden, piecing together the equipment you need, you will need to purchase lighting fixtures.

The most effective lighting for a hydroponics system is the High-Intensity Discharge (HID) light fixture made up of either Metal Halide (MH) bulbs or High-Pressure Sodium (HPS) bulbs. The HPS, in particular, emits a red or orange-looking light, which works well for plants, particularly in their vegetative growth stage.

Another type of lighting used is T5. It produces fluorescent light of a high output, and this lighting consumes low energy and only a little heat. The T5 is suitable for when growing plant cuttings, and for growing plants with short growth cycles.

Ensure that the light is kept on a time so that the lighting will go on and off at the same time, each day.

PH testing kit

If you don't test the pH of your nutrient solution from time to time, you will be running your farm purely by guesswork, subjecting your entire investment to a trial-and-error game. The reality is that for your plants to thrive in the hydroponic garden you have set up, there needs to be a balanced pH, and using a pH testing kit, you can regularly check on your garden to determine whether the pH of the nutrient solution is optimal. If the pH is too low, you can adjust by bringing it up, and if it's too high, you can lower it also.

On a related note, besides the pH meter, you will also need equipment to measure the temperature and the PPM of the water. You could also purchase the equipment you would need to measure the humidity and temperature of the grow room. If, for example, you find that you need to adjust the humidity in the room, use a dehumidifier or a humidifier, to ensure that the plants do not dry out and that they do not dampen.

A fan or any other equipment that can be used to improve the air circulation in the room would also be welcome. Although a small oscillating fan may work for a beginner, you will need a more sophisticated fan as your garden grows, one with an intake and an exhaust system.

The nutrient solution

While the nutrient solution is not a tool, you will need to set it aside as you set your tools aside, in readiness for the setup of your garden. As we have established many times so far, the nutrient solution will be the primary source of nutrients for your plants for them to thrive.

The nutrient solution provides three primary macronutrients that can be found in most fertilizers: potassium, phosphorus and nitrogen, and a host of 10 other micronutrients that may not be found in the fertilizers, yet the plants need them to survive, grow and reproduce. Some of these micronutrients include zinc, molybdenum, boron, copper, iron, chloride and manganese.

As a beginner, it may benefit you to purchase an already mixed solution offering a balance of all the nutrients mentioned above, but as you gain more experience, you will find it easier to mix create your own nutrient solution, one that will provide the plants with all the nutrients they require.

The fertilizers or nutrients used in the hydroponic system you can find in both dry and liquid forms, and there are both organic and synthetic kinds. Either type you choose will be dissolved in water to come up with the nutrient solution that we have associated with the hydroponic system severely.

As you look around the store, you will find that there are some specific fertilizers or nutrients specifically designed for hydroponic farming, and if you use them, you are bound to receive good results, provided you follow all instructions indicated on the packaging. Kindly avoid using standard soil fertilizers in a hydroponic system because their mixing formulas are specifically designed for garden soil, not for direct infusion into the roots as it happens in hydroponics.

While still on the point of hydroponic fertilizers, ensure that you choose the kind of hydroponic nutrient that is designed for your particular needs. For example, you will find that some fertilizers are designed for flowering plants, while others are good for promoting vegetative growth such as that used for lettuce. If you apply the latter to a flowering plant, you will promote the growth of the leaves rather than the formation, enlargement, and blossoming of flowers.

The quality of the water used

The solubility of water and its ability to deliver the nutrients you dissolved into it is affected both by the salt level of the water, as can be seen from the PPM, and the water pH. Typically, hard water has a high mineral content, and this fact keeps it from dissolving the minerals as effectively as the water that has a low mineral content. Therefore, in the event that the water you have for your project is hard, you will need to filter it out to take out the high mineral content.

The ideal water pH for making the nutrient solution is between 5.8 and 6.2, which is somewhat acidic. If your water is not at this pH level, you can use some chemicals to adjust it so that the pH gets within this ideal range.

The conditions of the room

It is of utmost importance, and great value, that the hydroponic system be set in the right conditions. Some of the elements you ought to check to ensure that the conditions are right include the carbon dioxide levels, relative humidity, temperature, and air circulation.

The humidity level is ideal if it ranges between 40% to 60% relative humidity. If the humidity gets to higher levels, it may lead to the formation of powdery mildew and other kinds of fungi.

The ideal temperature should range from 68 to 70F. If the temperatures are higher, the plants will become stunted, and if it gets even higher, the roots may start to rot.

The level of carbon dioxide, CO_2, is of most importance in the grow room. The best way to ensure that there is an adequate supply of it is by ensuring that the room has a free flow of air. As your farm or garden becomes bigger, you could now begin to supplement the CO_2 levels in the room because the more the gas is available in the growth room, the faster the growth of crops.

Chapter 4

Best plants for hydroponics gardening

It should be possible to grow almost anything hydroponically. After all, you are supplying all the nutrients the plant needs.

Here are the growth factors for plants.

- Temperature
- Humidity
- Nutrients
- Water
- Oxygen
- CO_2
- Wind
- Radiation (light)

Failing to supply one or more in this list will result in slower growth or a failed crop. Make sure you always have these eight elements optimized to have the quickest growing crop.

However, as with anything, some plants are better suited to this type of system, while others are not. Here are some that do exceptionally well in a hydroponic system:

Lettuce

This is potentially the easiest plant to grow and a great one for anyone new to hydroponics. They can adapt to any hydroponics system, need just ten to fourteen hours of light a day. They are surprisingly flexible regarding temperature. It prefers temperatures between 45°F and 70°F (7-21°C).

It is a fast-growing plant that will help you feel successful on your first try. You should plant them between six to eight inches (fifteen to twenty centimeters) apart. Lettuce does very well in Kratky, NFT, and deep-water culture.

Lettuce in an NFT system

Tomatoes

Tomatoes are an excellent choice for the Dutch bucket system. It should be noted that tomatoes prefer warmer weather. You may also need artificial lighting to ensure they have enough light. Besides, you'll need to use trellises because tomato plants will grow tall.

Removing suckers

To boost your yield and improve the quality of your tomato plant, it is a good idea to learn how to remove the suckers properly.

Each of the suckers will drain the energy from the main plant instead of allowing the nutrition to be absorbed. If you don't remove them, then you will have more foliage, which will lead to blockage of light to the flowering plant — actually reducing your yield compared to pruned suckers.

It is a good idea to do this when the sucker is small, it will minimize the risk of infection. Look for a place where more than one stem leaves the main stem. You will need to remove the middle stem, leaving just one.

Identifying a sucker on a tomato plant

It is also a good idea to remove any leaves that appear in the first two feet of the plant once it is matured. This will reduce the amount of diseases.

Spinach

Growing it hydroponically means you can grow it throughout the year. It is quite easy to grow, and very tolerant of temperature changes.

You should aim for the same spacing as lettuce, although you can plant a little denser if needed. It is comfortable in a temperature range of 50-80°F (10-27°C), making it easy to look after. Spinach takes about one and a half to two months to grow from seed to harvest. Spinach can be cut to regrow again up to three times.

Strawberry

Strawberries do exceptionally well in a hydroponics system. Unlike many fruit plants, they flourish throughout the year with minimum input.

Don't forget that if you start with seeds, it can take a long time before you to get any fruit.

It is normal to start from runners, which can be purchased throughout the year. They will need between eight to twelve hours of light per day and need temperatures between 60-80°F (15-27°C) with a slightly lower night temperature.

Bell peppers

Bell peppers need to be spaced eighteen to twenty-four inches apart to ensure the whole plant gets the nutrition and light it needs. The plant does need warmer temperatures like tomatoes, and you will need to provide trellises as the plants can get very heavy.

It is also a good idea to make sure they have between fourteen to eighteen hours of light every day.

These grow best in a dutch bucket system.

Arugula

You may know this as 'rocket salad' and be accustomed to including it in your salad.

You will find these are a good option for Kratky, NFT, or DWC systems.

Kale

This leafy vegetable is surprisingly easy to grow in your hydroponics system.

Kale does very well in a DWC system, Kratky, and NFT.

Herbs

Almost any herb will do well in a hydroponic system. For example, chives, mint, lavender, parsley, rosemary, basil, and coriander.

Herbs do very well in an NFT system. They respond well to the constant flow of water. Keep an eye on the roots, so they don't get too big and block the channel.

Flowers

Virtually any flower can be grown hydroponically. Although they may not give you edible produce, they can be sold. Especially as you can grow them all year round in a greenhouse.

Flowers of all shapes and sizes tend to do very well in a dutch bucket system and NFT depending on their size.

Plants to avoid

Here are the ones you should avoid trying to grow hydroponically:

Pumpkins

Pumpkins love sunshine and well-drained, pH-neutral soil.

Perhaps most importantly is the fact that they have large root clusters and spread quickly. Thus, making them difficult to grow in most hydroponic systems.

Squash

Squash grows at the base of the plant, which means it may be resting on damp growing media. This is likely to encourage fungal growth.

Besides, squash is generally a large plant with a minimal yield. There are much better ways to utilize the space in your hydroponics system.

Zucchini

This is a large plant, which means it will need plenty of support. It needs more nutrients than other plants, and will not give as great of a yield for the space.

You would need to maintain the temperature around 75°F (24°C), even throughout the night. It will also dry out very quickly if it doesn't get enough water and nutrients.

Potatoes

Most root vegetables are not well suited for hydroponic systems. Potatoes are such a case.

The cost of the crop will be low compared to your effort in growing it.

Radish

Some plants will grow well, but they are still not a good option, radish is one of these. You would need to choose the right media to grow these hydroponically, and you will find the cost is probably higher than purchasing it at the store.

Shrubs

This isn't what most people think of when starting a hydroponics system, but it is worth noting that shrubs, corn, and similar plants have a large root system. You would need a massive water reservoir and planting container to accommodate these needs which wouldn't be a viable option.

Chapter 5

----- ❧❦❧ -----

Hydroponics Vs soil gardening and & advantages and disadvantages

Hydroponics vs soil gardening

So, what makes hydroponics so different from traditional soil gardening methods? In this chapter, you are going to find out. Here are the advantages of each type of plant growing concept.

Areas where hydroponic gardening is better

•   Hydroponics prevents the overuse of fertilizer. Hydroponic plants are grown in a very controlled environment, where waste products are limited and less nutrient material is needed. The great thing about this control is that it allows less fertilizer to be used. This is especially beneficial for the humans and animals in the area, who will have less of a chance of drinking fertilizer-contaminated water.

•   Hydroponics make better use of space and location. You can grow an indoor hydroponics system anywhere that you have room, because it takes up so little space and everything that the plant needs can be provided by your system. Additionally, roots grown in the soil need room to spread out while plants grown hydroponically have root systems that do not need to spread out. This means that you can grow plants closer together and save space.

• Hydroponics uses less water. You would think that a hydroponic growing system would use more water than traditional methods, but that is not true. When plants are grown hydroponically, they are given only the amount of water that they need. When you water plants that are in soil, some of the water is going to seep into the ground or leak out of the pot. It will also be evaporated. Therefore, the plants are actually receiving only a fraction of the water that you are providing. Hydroponic systems are much more efficient when it comes to water usage and you actually end up using 70 to 80 percent less water.

• Hydroponics systems reduce weeds, pests, and diseases. When you use more traditional gardening methods, the soil that you grow in can be filled with diseases, pests, and other plant parts. Hydroponic systems do away with this problem almost entirely.

• Hydroponic systems grow plants twice as fast as traditional methods. Do you know what that means? You can have more harvests each year. Because hydroponic systems provide exactly what the plant needs without the plant having to hunt for it, the growing cycle is much more efficient.

• Hydroponics makes it easier for you to tamper with the nutrients for growing. Every plant, like every person, is unique. Each type is going to thrive in certain environments and struggle in others. Hydroponics is fun in this way. You have the ability to adjust the amount of nutrients in the solution and adjust it until you have the perfect growth solution.

Areas where soil gardening is better

•   Soil gardening has a lower initial cost. While hydroponics systems vary in their initial cost, they can get quite expensive. Some of this cost will be offset by the lesser amount of water, fertilizer, and pesticides that you will need.

•   Soil gardening does not use electricity. In several hydroponics gardening techniques, you must use a light source. Additionally, some systems use electricity to create bubbles in the nutrient system to aerate the roots.

•   Soil gardening has a less risk of mold and bacteria growth. One disadvantage of hydroponics is that plants are grown in a very moist environment. This leaves the plants susceptible to growth of mold and sometimes dangerous bacteria if enough precautions are not taken.

Now that you have an understanding of the major ways that hydroponics differs from more traditional growing methods using soil, it is time to move on.

Advantages and disadvantages

Any system of growing produce is going to have advantages and disadvantages. It is a good idea to be aware of what these are before you start your DIY system. We will begin by looking at the advantages.

The advantages

Grow anywhere

There are large areas of the world that can't be used to grow food, specifically deserts and dry regions. But, providing you can get water to these places, you can set up a hydroponics system and grow crops.

Considering much of the space in a dessert is classified as 'useless,' that is a real bonus! It doesn't even matter what the soil is made of.

Fewer pests

Soil-borne pests often attack plants. Because soil is not an essential part of a hydroponics system, the risk of disease is reduced. It should be noted that it is not eliminated as airborne pests can still introduce diseases to your hydroponics system.

Greenhouses or indoor growing setups act as a barrier for pests. One of the advantages of a greenhouse is that you can release beneficial insects that eat pests. If you are using a greenhouse, these beneficial insects are contained.

Faster growing time

Plants that are grown in hydroponics will grow more quickly because they have access to all the nutrients and trace elements. They provide more yield and are more pest resistant. In short, hydroponics gives better results than conventional farming methods.

Research shows that lettuce grown hydroponically can yield as much as eighty-eight pounds/ ten feet squared (forty-one kilograms/meter squared) a year. As opposed to just eight and a half pounds/ ten feet squared (three point nine kilograms/meter squared) a year when grown conventionally.

Water usage was ten times lower with hydroponics than soil-grown crops. Harvest was 11 times greater with hydroponics than soil.

These numbers seem to speak for themselves, but you have additional costs when doing hydroponics, which have to be factored in. In this study, they also calculated that the energy cost was 82 times greater in hydroponics than soil. This is very important to know for commercial operations.

Better Control

Hydroponics farming allows you to monitor and adjust the nutrients in the water. This gives you much more control over the growing environment, helping to produce the best possible yield in the shortest possible time.

Water Usage

Research concludes that hydroponics uses ninety percent less water than growing plants conventionally in the field. This is because the water is re-circulated most of the times, water is only lost through evaporation or a water exchange.

The disadvantages

With the advantages, you will always have disadvantages.

Let's look at them next.

High set-up costs

Hydroponics has higher start-up costs than soil-grown crops. This is because you need several items to start with:

- A water tank

- A pump to re-circulate the water
- A setup for your plants to grow (NFT, DWC)
- A grow medium
- The need to buy nutrients
- Sometimes artificial light sources

Airborne diseases

Although the risk of soil-based diseases is lower, air-borne diseases can happen, and because of the nature of hydroponics, these diseases can quickly spread between plants because they are planted closer to each other.

It is essential to be aware of the main signs of plant disease and react a fast as possible.

Another example of a disease that is not airborne is Pythium (root rot), which can be introduced to a hydroponic system through the water and will result in browning of the roots. Luckily, you can control most of these by proper design of the system, which we will talk about later in the book.

Knowledge

Understanding the principles behind hydroponics is relatively straightforward, although some learning is necessary. However, to properly run the system, you need to understand the different pieces of equipment involved and how to monitor and adjust nutrient levels.

Getting this right is essential to creating a long-lasting system, but it can be a steep learning curve. If you are not having success from the first time, see it as a learning experience and not as a defeat.

Monitoring

If you grow crops using conventional soil-based methods, you'll be able to leave your plants for several days. Nature has a habit of finding a way to help plants grow in almost any situation.

If you've created a hydroponics system, you should check for visible problems and check the nutrient levels quite often.

Having a mechanical failure can have an extremely negative effect on your hydroponics system, potentially killing your plants!

Of course, there are several ways to automate parts of the system, but this should not be your primary concern when you create your first hobby system.

Electricity

Electricity is essential to run the pumps, supply artificial light, heating or cooling, and air movement. All these additions will result in a higher electrical bill, which is an additional cost.

Water and electricity do not generally mix well, making this a safety risk that you need to be aware of.

If anything happens to the electricity supply, your plants can suffer surprisingly quickly. You should have a back-up option to run the pump for a few hours in a commercial system. This can be done with a solar setup or a backup generator.

Chapter 6

Myths and mistakes to avoid

Myths

Hydroponics is a new technology

This is a very common myth that is very popular amongst the traditionalists among us. However, as said earlier, it is just a myth. Hydroponic gardening is a very old and ancient field. It is believed that the pharaohs of Egypt loved fruits and vegetables that were grown hydroponically. Even the famous wonder of the Ancient World, The Hanging Gardens of Babylon, were supposed to be hydroponic gardens. In India, plants are grown directly in a coconut husk; hydro at the most grassroots level. It is thus proven that hydroponic gardening is not at all a new technique but an old and ancient science of cultivation.

Hydroponics is artificial or unnatural

Once again, this myth is highly popular amongst the traditional thinkers. Such people think that growing plants in water is against nature and is artificial. This is absolute rubbish. The growth of plants is a real and naturally occurring thing and cannot be done artificially. Plants need certain things to grow and thrive and they normally take these things from the soil. In hydroponics, we just replace the soil with water. Plants still can absorb whatever they need from the water and grow well. Unless you consider water unnatural, then you simply cannot consider hydroponic gardening unnatural.

Hydroponic gardening does not involve any kind of genetic mutation or introduction of any unwarranted and mysterious chemicals. This is not a steroid inducing system but is a perfectly natural and safe method of growing crops.

Hydroponics harms the environment

This is a ridiculous myth. Hydroponic gardening does not harm the environment at all. In fact, it helps the environment. Water is one of our most precious resources and because of hydroponic gardening, around 70 to 90 % of water can be saved as compared to the conventional form of gardening. Hydroponic gardening also does not have any fertilizer runoff. This runoff can pollute the soil and rivers, lakes, etc.

Hydroponics is Very Complicated and Cannot Be Done At Home Unless You Are Exceptionally Talented

Hydroponics is a very easy system of gardening that can be done by almost anyone with a love of plants. An inexpensive hydroponic system can be constructed with simple things such as a bucket, hydroponic growing medium, and hydroponic nutrients. You can definitely use advanced technology and science to create an exceptionally sophisticated hydroponic garden to produce high amounts of yield but you can also use simple, cheap, yet effective instruments and equipment if you want to do hydroponic gardening just as a hobby. As said earlier anyone can pick up hydroponic gardening, anyone means people of all ages.

Hydroponics is far too expensive

You can definitely use expensive and advanced technology and science to create an exceptionally sophisticated hydroponic garden to produce high amounts of yield but you can also use simple, cheap, yet effective instruments and equipment if you want to do hydroponic gardening just as a hobby. You can work on a limited budget yet produce excellent and fantastic results with ease if you are dedicated to your garden.

Not widespread and limited to developed nations

This is a rather bizarre and ridiculous myth. Hydroponic gardening is done in every corner of the world.

People do hydroponic gardening in places where the climate is unsuitable for the growth of plants or in nations where the quality of soil is not suitable for a good yield. It is also commonly used in developed and developing nations such as the USA where the soil has been abused and is no longer cultivable. In British Columbia, 90% of all the greenhouse industry is now based upon the hydroponic gardening system.

Hydroponics must be done indoors

Hydroponics is generally cultivated indoors because people have no place to cultivate plants outside, but relax. You can easily grow a hydroponic garden outdoors as well. A benefit of constructing a hydroponic garden indoors is the fact that you can control the lights. Outdoors you need to depend on the sun for the light. It not impossible or hard to do hydroponic gardening outdoors. It is even possible to do soil gardening inside the house if you know how to do it.

Hydroponics don't need pesticides

Well this myth is very common but unfortunately false. You do need pesticides for a hydroponic garden, but the soil-born pests are eliminated naturally because of there being no soil. There are other kinds of pests that you need to protect your plants from. You should ideally only use pesticides when you feel that your plants are under attack. To avoid the attack of pests, keep a close eye on your system. Never enter the dark room when you are unclean or have come from outdoors especially from a garden or a park.

Hydroponics produce huge plants

This myth is slightly true. Every seed like every other living thing has a genetic code that has all the coding that determines the size, weight, yield, etc. of the plant that the seed will produce. Hydroponics is a well-developed system, but it is not a magical system that can force a seed of cherry tomato to grow a beefsteak tomato plant. Yes, it can help you to grow the best cherry tomatoes with the seed though.

It is quite hard to grow a seed to its highest point in soil as the makeup of the soil varies from place to place. Although the components of the soil can be controlled and manipulated, you cannot have 100% control over them. However, in the case of hydroponic gardening you have total control and freedom on the components. You can easily manipulate them, so as to grow the best plants easily. Hydroponic gardening also consumes a lesser amount of energy as compared to soil gardening. This reserved energy is used by the plants to produce more and more yield. The plants become healthy, their foliage is dense and their flower and fruits delightful.

Hydroponics is used primarily for illegal purposes

This myth, unfortunately, has some truth in it. However, like every other thing in this world, you can use hydroponics for a good purpose as well as a bad purpose. Sugar is a very tasty and sweet product but if used wrongly, it can give you diabetes. Similarly, dynamite is a very useful product but if used in an improper way, it can be dangerous. Hydroponic gardening is no different. Often, law enforcement officials talk about hydroponic gardening when talking about marijuana and such illegal substances. Many people thus form a relationship or connection between two things and start believing that hydroponics is exclusively used to grow illegal substances. Yes, it is true that people do use hydroponic systems for illegal purposes, but people use cars for illegal purposes too. If you cannot stop using cars, you should not stop using hydroponic gardening as an alternative kind of gardening. Remember, any power is good only until it is in safe hands. Power itself is not corrupt. The people who use it are corrupt. Likewise, hydroponic gardening is not wrong or illegal. The corrupt people who use it for their illegal benefits are wrong.

Mistakes

Since you are just now getting into hydroponics gardening, you may want to take things as slowly and as carefully as you could. One mistake could send the entire project rolling down the hill, and no one wants that. What an investment you have made, and how sad it would be to see it all amount to nothing! What you do to prevent this is to get first, a clear understanding of what your intended plants expect of you and how to attend to each of their needs.

While knowing what to do is important, you should also beware of what not to do, because doing so would mess up your project. Below is a review of common mistakes beginner hydroponic gardeners can make:

#1: Going cheap by sourcing ineffective or not buying enough lighting

One of the most critical investments you ought to make as a hydroponic farmer is to seek the best lighting for your crops. This requires you to conduct first, substantial research in the market, and among seasoned hydroponic farmers, on the right kind of lighting, bearing in mind that different bulbs will produce different kinds of energy and light spectrums.

Also, don't expect that placing your plants next to a window is enough substitution for grow lights because usually, the light that gets in through the window is not sufficient, or strong enough to support the vigorous growth common among hydroponic plants.

#2: Designing unusable or difficult-to-use hydroponic farms

Some beginners make the mistake of designing an unusable farm because they lack experience or because they have not dealt with hydroponics before, at least not on a large scale.

Due to inexperience, they fail to think about factors like efficiency and workflow, which leads to farms that make regular maintenance operations difficult, make harvesting difficult and do not use the space available efficiently. These inefficient gardens may also demand lots of tending, transplanting due to death of the plants, and difficulties controlling pests. Farmers also have a difficult time accessing various parts of the systems.

Now that labor is the most expensive variable cost in a farm, it is of great importance that the farms have labor-efficient designs.

The solution to this mistake is to take some considerable time to plan out and think about how the system will work, and from there, you can now build individual components. Consider all the variables, including water, nutrients, light, pests, convenience, access, redundancy, and automation, right from the start, and only start planning out the design once you have figured out each of the variables mentioned.

It would help if you went benchmarking, by visiting and talking to seasoned growers to see the systems they are operating. Go ahead and ask questions, including seeking answers to the question of what they would do differently were they to turn back and begin afresh.

#3: Confusing biological viability with economic viability

One of the misconceptions flying around the agricultural product markets is that establishing a farm requires 90% growing while selling takes 10%. However, when it comes to reality, the opposite is true, and many farmers make mistakes on either of the systems.

The farmers fail to take into consideration the financial costs and the time it would take for them to get their produce to the market once it has matured, and because of this small omission, many do not budget either money or the time that they would need to get their produce to the consumers. This effectively disrupts the schedule they had previously set for the farm and can lead to frustration due to lack of a market.

The second batch are those that go-ahead to plan for the biological functions of their farms, including the crops to grow, the techniques to use, and the equipment to source for, but they do all this without testing the feasibility of what they are producing in the market. They are not careful to ensure that what they are producing matches the local demand. In the end, the farmers are frustrated at having a lot of produce and a facility, with no consumers to buy what they have grown.

The bottom line is that it will not matter how much effort you have dedicated to your farm, or how healthy and better tasting they are if no one wants them.

#4: Underestimating the cost of crop production and of purchasing the hydroponic system

It is typical of many motivated and determined hydroponic beginners to be so excited about getting into the hydroponic business that they underestimate just how they would have to spend to succeed at it. Beginners are often asked to start small and scale to bigger establishments with time, even if they feel like they have the resources they would need to go big. The problem is that some do not heed this instruction, and instead, they enter the industry and purchase large facilities, equipment, and expensive utilities.

Unfortunately, those who go ahead to start their gardens find that the costs of running hydroponic gardens are way too high, and some may quit in the middle of it due to the inadequacy of resources. Others do not even get to start the production process because by the time they finish purchasing the equipment and other resources, they no longer have any money to move ahead. The result is that in either case, the farmers do not get the chance to utilize their equipment fully due to unanticipated costs.

Therefore, as you make plans for your intended project, keep in mind costs like pest control, heat removal, replacement of equipment, labor, insurance, packaging, ongoing maintenance, and the cost of printing marketing materials. All these costs add up to a significant amount.

The most critical of the costs that are often underestimated is the cost of labor, whether the farmer is providing it himself or hiring someone to do it. If you are producing in rafts, for example, realize that it is a labor-intensive hydroponic production practice. The cost of labor for raft systems can go up to 45% or 60% of the total production costs. Many producers do not even take notice of this when calculating and making their estimates. Therefore, when they get to the harvesting and processing stages, they are left in shock, not believing what their returns have become.

#5: Choosing the wrong market

The market for which you are producing is another critical factor that you ought to consider, whether your project is producing food to be sold later, or to be consumed by your family. If you grow crops that your market does not want, you will be wasting resources and opportunity. The result is that you will be trying to push your products on unwilling consumers, leading to wastage, and a loss of resources because you will not get a return on your investment.

Some crops are easy to grow, and when they are grown under hydroponics, their production is especially high. However, the crops are just unwanted. Therefore, before you decide on the crop you want to grow, conduct a proper analysis of your market, and even so, look at what your competition is growing. From there, come up with something that will give you lots of customers.

If you are living in an area where field producers present fierce competition with their produce, choose to produce what the producers cannot grow in that period. In most cases, if a consumer, say a restaurant, wants to buy organic lettuce and the field producer offers it at 50 cents a pound, the field producer will have the attention of the consumer, at least for the summer period, when he is producing.

When the seasonal competition is too stiff, come up with ways to survive and not lose your spot in the market. If you prove to be reliable, you will win the loyalty of many consumers, and you can lock them into permanent purchasing contracts, such that they will not even consider other producers, cheaper or not.

Chapter 7

Growing mediums & nutrients and lights

The combination of 3

Like any other system, hydroponics system is also a great combination of various equipment and elements. The process of hydroponic involves the soilless growing of plants with the help of water, nutrient solutions, light and many other things like water pump which generate the oxygen and tubes which is very useful for dripping water and nutrients in the roots of plants.

The growing mediums are those which things which provide external support to the plant's roots like sand or clay. And nutrient solutions are immensely responsible for the healthy and rapid growth of the plant. And in terms of lighting, these are artificial lights which work as the permanent back up of natural sunlight for the plant.

Overall, these three contributes a lot to growing a healthy and organic plant. SO, let's check out them thoroughly and figure out their types and essentiality-

Nutri

Nutrient solutions are one of the most significant parts of the hydroponic system or soilless growing process. These nutrient solutions are readily available in gardening centers, nurseries, and any farming shops. Nutrient solutions are a mixture of many nutrients like potassium, magnesium, calcium, nitrogen, and many other minerals.

However, the use of the nutrients solution solely depends on the types of plants we are growing and what sort of medium and hydroponic system we are using. Though, the nutrients must be mixed or soluble in water only then they will work or produce results. On the other hand, the composition of nutrient solution is essential, and 20 above elements will be needed to grow a plant healthy. Though, oxygen, carbon, and hydrogen are consumed from the air and water.

And rest of the nutrients elements are known as a mineral nutrient that will be dissolved by the grower, and they needed to be in an appropriate ratio. An excellent hydroponic nutrient consists of nutrients like nitrogen, copper, zinc, iron, Sulphur, Molybdenum, magnesium, potassium, chlorine, and boron.

Grow

The growing mediums are work as a supporting system for plant roots. Because in soilless growing you can have the support of soil, that is why you need something to give the necessary support to plant roots in a hydroponic system.

However, the soilless growing can be done with or without growing medium but in the case where a growing medium is going to be used, then you can several choices, but they have their advantages and drawbacks. So, let's figure out some ever-increasing medium and also know about their benefits and disadvantages-

1) Rockwool

Rockwool is one of the most famous and most used growing media in hydroponic systems. They are sterile and non-degradable growing medium. They are primarily composed into limestone and then heated to make them small threads. After that, they are formed into sheets, blocks, slabs, etc. They are water absorbent and can quickly suffocate the roots.

2) Grow rock

It is another popular and immensely used growing medium in the hydroponic growing. Grow rock is lightweight expanded clay aggregate that is extremely heated to make a porous form or texture. These are considered heavy enough to support the plants, but still, show the quality of being lightweight. Grow rock is a non-degradable and sterile medium that contains a neutral PH. It is reusable and easily clean medium. But if you are planning to use it, then it would be quite time-consuming.

3) Coco fiber and chips

The coir and chips are the outer husk or exterior of coconut. Earlier, they were considered as the waste material which cannot be used further, and they also decompose slowly. But now they have become the best growing medium of hydroponic growing. Coco coir is pH neutral and contains moisture well. They come in two forms- Coco fiber and chips. The main difference between the two is their particle size. Coco fiber has a massive particle in comparison to chips.

4) Perlite

It is solely composed of minerals and subjected to high heat. Because after facing heat, perlite stretched out like popcorn and will become the lightweight absorbent and porous. It has a neutral PH level and high wicking system. It can be used solely or with other growing medium. Because of the lightweight quality, it is generally not suited for the flood and drain system.

5) Vermiculite

The vermiculite has similarities like perlite because it can also expand and faces high heat. It has several similarities to perlite except for great cation-exchange ability. It means vermiculite can hold nutrients for later use too. It also has lightweight quality and can be afloat. It comes in various types; that is why you need to identify first before purchasing.

6) Oasis cubes

Oasis cubes can absorb water and air easily because they are material of an open cell. They have similar properties like Rockwool; that is why they don't turn in to waterlogged cubes. These cubes are more like white floral foam which used to hold the stem in the flower display.

7) Floral foam

These foams can also be used as a growing medium in hydroponic growing. These are similar to oasis cubes, but the cell size is bigger in the floral foam. There are some drawbacks in floral foam. They can crumble easily and leave foam particles in the water. And second, they can also do the damage in the form of water-logging growing medium.

8) Grow stone hydroponic substrate

Grow stones medium are made up of recycled glass. These are lightweight, reusable, and unevenly shaped. They can provide significant moisture and air to the plant roots and also have excellent wicking ability.

9) River rock

River rock can easily be purchased through home stores. They are cheaper and come in different sizes. They have small edges and rounded shape. However, you need to sanitize them before using. They can give plenty amount of oxygen to the plant roots because they have air pockets.

10) Pine shaving

The commercial growers drastically use pine shaving as a growing medium. They do not have any chemical fungicides because they are made up of kiln-dried wood. They have a large air pocket that means great for air passing, but these can quickly cause waterlogged.

11) Composted and aged pine bark

Pine bark was among the first growing medium used in the hydroponic system. Pine bark used to consider as a water material, but now they are the best among other growing mediums. They have less organic acid property.

12) Polyfoam insulation

These are the alternative form of rock wool or oasis cubes because they are not often used in hydroponics as a growing medium. These are mainly termed as furniture foam. Poly foams come in different sizes and thickness.

13) Water absorbing crystals

These are mostly used in the commercial industry. These water absorbing crystals are used in separate area like a baby's diaper to the sports industry. They can expand drastically and soak water immensely. They are usable and cheaper.

14) Sand

Sand is a quite common growing medium in soilless growing. Sand is often mixed with coco coir, perlite and vermiculite to make out the best. Moisture doesn't come out quickly from the sand. Sand is the best way to pass out the aeration for the plant's roots.

Light

Plants require light for performing the process of photosynthesis. And where the natural light is not available or less the new use of artificial light like high-intensity discharge. There are two types of light metal halides and high-pressure sodium. So, let's check out some primary lighting system-

1) Metal halide bulbs

Metal halide bulb much emulates harsh sunlight. And that is why through these bulbs plant can easily do their photosynthesis process. Halide bulb technology is the best for growing a fast and healthier plant for gardening and farming.

2) High-pressure sodium bulb

High-pressure sodium lights specifically show high range in red and yellow regions of the spectrum. These light bulbs have a longer life than the previous lamps.

3) LED grow lights

Plant roots more respond to the LED lights. Through LED lights, plants grow healthier, internal nodal growth. LED lights are not suitable for big plants.

4) High output Fluorescents

These lights produce less heat in compassion to other lights that is you can grow or place the plants near the lights. They are best for seedling and do not generate noise, vibration, and heat.

5) Compact fluorescent lights

Compact fluorescent lamps are best in small places, and the best part is that they do not produce much heat and electricity. For flowering or fruiting the plants, you can use 2700k bulb. And when you are adjusting the light for taller plants (more than a foot), then you can also use standard fluorescent as a supplementary light.

Chapter 8

System maintenance

Tidy up the grow room in advance. Likewise, before setting up your system and returning it in the grow room, clean the plant box thoroughly with a 10% blanch arrangement. Continuously cut off dead leaves and expel them from the grow room. The rotting fundamental issue draws in growth gnats. You ought to likewise evacuate unhealthy plants, so the disease doesn't spread. At the point when you change the water in your repository, wash the tank thoroughly with a 10% fade arrangement. On the off chance that you utilize huge plate for your squares and sections, consider washing these as well, particularly on the off chance that you have had a problem with root spoil.

Drippers

If you utilize a drip system, purchase a couple of additional drippers, so you can change drippers if any are obstructed. Have a container with vinegar in your grow room and toss the obstructed drippers in so that they will be cleaned.

Ebb/Flo

We suggest that you get a clock that can be set at brief interims so that a full cycle will drench the stone fleece for 10 minutes. To maintain a strategic distance from salt developed, we recommend that you top water your plants once every week. Utilize a similar arrangement as in your supply.

Try not to topwater with plain water because it will stun your plants.

Additionally, make sure to have a plate with profound enough depressions, so water empties away out of the GRODAN solid shapes/sections.

Ph

Never go underneath pH 5, or the stone fleece might be harmed! Beneath pH 5 and higher than pH 7, the plant can't promptly take up nutrients.

1-2 hours before planting, remember to immerse the stone fleece with pH 5.5 water.

Flush GRODAN with your nutrient arrangement at pH 5.5 and channel to waste and afterward put the GRODAN in your system.

The pH in your repository will go up during vegetative growth- it is a typical reaction - it implies your plant is growing! Yet, also, higher temperatures and green growth in your supply will make pH go up. So watch out for pH. For most plants, the supply ought to associate with pH 6.0

Supply Solution

You can top up the supply and modify EC/pH, yet your answer might be out of small-scale nutrients or be contaminated with Pythium (root spoil). On the off chance that your store contains prepared to utilize (weakened) nutrient arrangement, it would be ideal if you utilize phosphoric corrosive (pH Down) or lemon juice to bring down pH.

Hydroponic System activity cycle

Together with the cleansing of the nutrient arrangement, the significance of the previously mentioned parts of hydroponic practice is usually terribly thought little of, and, without due accentuation, significant and steady outcomes won't be accomplished.

Outright tidiness of the growing region is an absolute necessity to accomplish the highest growth and least problems from pests and diseases. In this way, sick foliage ought to be speedily expelled from plants and, alongside general flotsam and jetsam, expelled from the growing zone, with surfaces kept clean from the residue, earth, and spillages. Limiting workforce traffic in the region, no smoking, and sifting the air supply to the region are other beneficial precautionary measures.

Nutrient cleansing

It's entirely expected to hear gardeners censuring their nutrients for poor growth results. However, as a rule, the genuine reason is the failure to purify the nutrient arrangement.

Not at all, like soil culture, hydroponic nutrient arrangements are presented to the environment and are an ideal reproducing ground for some types of infection (for example, pythium, fusarium). To forestall malady entrance, the nutrient arrangement, medium, roots (and so forth.) ought to be consistently cleaned.

'Sanitizing operators' must yield a remaining concoction when broken up in the working nutrient with the goal that the whole system is dealt with each time plants are watered. Verifiably, chlorine dioxide, sodium hypochlorite, and monochloramine are utilized for this reason. However, monochloramine has the benefit of having a long half-life, is delicate on roots, and is good with the majority of the 'natural' mediums and growth advertisers utilized in hydroponics.

Supplanting Nutrients

In recycling hydroponic systems, the nutrient arrangement must be consistently supplanted. That is, it ought to be depleted and supplanted with new nutrients. This is done to keep up the nutrient's adjust and forestall the development of aggravation and destructive salts (for example, sodium, chloride), pathogen, soil, and so on.

In both winter and summer, by and massive dump somewhere around at regular intervals. The dumping recurrence can be less if utilizing precipitation or RO (turn around assimilation) water.

Salty water: More regular dumping (for example, at regular intervals) might be vital when utilizing salty make-up water since synthetic disturbance compounds develop all the more quickly to poisonous/precipitation levels – particularly during sweltering, dry climate.

The technique for dumping: Poorly planned equipment can make dumping a dreary and chaotic assignment with the end goal that there is a compulsion to defer or perform less now and again than should be expected. So consider this at the plan organize – or before you purchase. Sadly, most system plans are not thought about the issues of dumping. Consider the benefits of the accompanying plan highlights:

1.Introduce an in-line 2-path valve between the siphon and feed outlets to redirect the nutrient flow to squander.

2.In a perfect world, structure a slanting floor into the tank, which channels towards a sump from which the nutrient is depleted. This will help evacuate the last hardly any liters containing the more significant part of the dregs. Another less complicated technique can be to tilt the tank towards the outlet.

3.'Sump' siphons are advantageous for depleting tanks. They are light, convenient, and simple to prime; however, they will ordinarily deplete to a profundity of around 1 inch. Henceforth, a slanting tank floor or implicit sump is required for the best outcomes.

Where to dump: Utilize the staying wholesome advantage by setting it on your garden or applying over a vast region of prairie, and so forth. Try not to put down channels, toilets, or in conduits or fill sand as this can cause ecological harm (for example, green growth blossom).

Flushing of the root zone with new water

Hydroponic systems must be consistently flushed and cleaned with new water. (Likewise, note that for ailment control, outer equipment tidiness is as significant as within tanks/channels.) This is done to evacuate the development of an excessive amount of calcium (white encourages – causing blockages) and undesirable/unsafe salts (for example sodium, chloride), root exudates, green growth, pathogens, and so on from the root zone, medium and other system parts.

Give specific consideration to the flushing of the root zone and feed circuit. Further, examine channels, gulfs, and outlets, and so on before recharging the system with crisp nutrients since they are inclined to get hindered with durable material removed during the flushing procedure.

Re-coursing systems: Flushing is done quickly following each dumping cycle. Initially, do any essential manual cleaning, for example, expel any conspicuous development, and so on. Halfway fill the supply with crisp water. At that point, work the siphon with the point of flushing the feed circuit and root zone/medium (flushing can be improved by showering with a garden hose). Dispose of waste utilizing the strategies prompted for dumping. Rehash process until squander water is transparent, and conductivity is near that of the makeup water.

Rush to-squander systems: Although it is generally necessary for some specialists to flush just every 7-14 days, some business growers think of it as essential to flush day by day! The recurrence eventually relies upon saltiness, temperature, medium, plant assortment, and different variables.

Flushing techniques are:

a) If flushing can be booked to happen when the working nutrient tank is unfilled (for example, between nutrient bunches), at that point, the current system equipment can be used. Spot low alkalinity* water in the store and work the nutrient siphon until the EC of the run-off water is fundamentally lower than the typical working EC or no higher than ~0.5mS over that of the water in the repository. Where the outside of the medium is promptly open, it tends to be advantageous to do extra flushing with a garden hose.

* Lower the pH of faucet water to ~5.0. RO or downpour water won't require altering.

b) If flushing should be directed more routinely than in the situation above, at that point, a similar system applies. However, it will be essential to have a committed repository and siphon for flushing. This can be associated with the current feed circuit at an intersection controlled by a 2-way valve. This valve is redirected to this repository to apply flushing at whatever point flushing happens.

Post collect tidy up.

Two separate strategies are required to guarantee equipment is perfect preceding replanting:

Malady Prevention

Toward the finish of each harvest, it is essential to disinfect the whole hydroponic system to help forestall sickness problems in the following yield. The accompanying aide will help expel natural develop from pathogen, green growth, sludges, and dead/rotting plant matter:

Stage 1. Evacuate all plants and media, at that point, do, however, much manual cleaning as could reasonably be expected. Extreme tidiness is as significant as inward.

Stage 2. Mostly fill the system with water. Lower the water's pH to beneath 5, at that point, with curbed light conditions, include family unit chlorine bleach** (50g/L chlorine) at ~5ml per liter (4 tsp per gallon).

Stage 3. Blend well, at that point drench system for 24-72 hours. (Note that chlorine fade won't break down green growth or durable general material.

Just wet brushing will evacuate those contaminants.) Suitable treatment over that time incorporates:

✓ For re-coursing systems, run the siphon for at any rate 15 minutes consistently.

✓ For hurry to-squander systems, run the siphon for a short burst once consistently.

Stage 4. A while later, dispose of this arrangement, at that point, flush the entire system a few times with little volumes of crisp water to expel all hints of chlorine, ousted material, and so on.

Stage 5. Where fine drippers, sprayers, etc. are utilized, it might be essential to disassemble and clean every unit independently.

Encourage Removal

Over the long haul, it is once in a while valuable to lead an acid** flush to help expel accelerates (white hastens of calcium sulfate and phosphate that can't be broken up with plain water or wet brushing.

Stage 1. Initially, treat the system as nitty-gritty for "malady counteraction" above.

Stage 2. To tank, include water and enough hydrochloric corrosive to accomplish pH 2. For instance: if utilizing precipitation or RO water, weaken 30% (for example, typical business quality) by around one thousand overlays or 1 ml for each liter (3/4 tsp per gallon).

Stage 3. Splash system for 24-72 hours. Appropriate strategies may include:

✓ For re-flowing systems, run the siphon for in any event 15 minutes consistently.

✓ For race to-squander systems, run the siphon for a short burst once consistently and gather the release.

Stage 4. After that, kill arrangement up to pH 5-6 with soft drink debris before disposing of.

Stage 5. Flush the entire system a few times with crisp water to evacuate all hints of corrosive, ousted material, and so forth.

Stage 6. Where fine drippers, sprayers, etc. are utilized, it might be essential to destroy and clean every unit independently.

Be sure to follow essential security safeguards and contact no metal parts.

Chapter 9

----- ~~~ -----

Problems with the operation of a hydroponic system

Because hydroponic plants can be completely sealed off from the environment by installation in greenhouses, problems with plant pests are much lower than in conventional fields.

However, other difficulties arise: due to the often warm temperatures in the greenhouses and (especially with the dripping method) many thin lines, the water heats up quickly. This reduces the possibility of binding oxygen and co2.

Biofilms are another problem—slimy forms of algae, protozoa, and fungi that form quite quickly. These plaques can clog parts of the irrigation system, causing crop failures. Besides, biofilms are an excellent reservoir for bacteria and fungi that can damage the roots of plants.

Algae in hydroponic

Algae can be a problem in any type of hydroponics. In a bubbler system, it often takes place in the nutrient reservoir, especially when the container lets in light. Building up algae reduces the nutrients in the system, which makes the plants work harder as they compete with the algae for food. Algae can also coat the airstone, which is the part of the system that creates the bubbles. The thicker the algae become, the more difficult it is for bubbles to escape, resulting in reduced oxygenation of the water.

Possible diseases and pests in indoor plants

Houseplants with hard leaves are less susceptible to pests, as they cannot easily grip the leaf. Therefore, it is particularly effective in these plants to spray the plant simply with a hard water-steel. In plants such as a sansevieria or the chamaerops humilis, you can occasionally inject with a pressure sprayer now and then as a preventative measure. Specific information on certain pests, vermin species, diseases, or pests can be found here:

- Spider mites
- Scale lice
- Wolllaus

SPIDER MITES

Spider mites are an infection of mites on the plant. Characteristic of the spinnmilde is the small, pear-shaped body, which is about as big as a pinhead. If plants are affected by spider mites, they are deprived of the necessary nutrients.

Variants of the pest

Spider mites are available in many different variations, most of which are plant-specific. For example, the common spider mite is common in greenhouses.

Susceptible plants

Depending on the spider mite species, other plants are susceptible. Examples of susceptible plants are the alocasia and the polyscias. Above all, however, plants that are often in dry soil are the most susceptible to an infection of spider mites.

Place of infestation

The spider mites often sit under the leaves. Since they are very small and move little, but they are difficult to discover.

Appearance

The spider mites are about 0.3 and 0.5mm in size and have a pear-shaped body. Depending on the species, spider mites have a brown, red or yellow-green color. The best way to recognize a spider mite infestation on the leaves of plants. Because these get brown, almost coppery points and after a while yellow or brown and fall off. In the case of a longer infestation, a white tissue often appears on the underside of the leaves.

Reason

Like other mite species, spider mites also become active in warm and dry weather. Often spider mites also occur through old soil. Because of the earth no longer has any nutrients, this is the perfect place for the spider mite to develop. Since even weak plants are frequently attacked, it often helps to repot the plant and thereby give it energy and resistance again.

Distribution

Spider mites benefit from their size and agility. This allows spider mites to reproduce easily through plant-to-plant contact.

Damage to the plant

Spider mites poke small holes in the leaves, sucking nutrients out of the plant. As a result, the plant can no longer transport or absorb nutrients and will most likely die from prolonged infestation. If the spider mite is not fought well and on time, it becomes a pretty stubborn plague for any plant.

Fighting

Prevention is easier than getting rid of it. Therefore, we recommend occasionally spraying your plants with pesticides. You can also prevent infestation by spraying with water, as spider mites prefer a dry environment. There are several ways to fight spider mites. First of all, we recommend removing the affected leaves and branches. Do not try to touch the healthy branches with the affected branches. In case of heavy infestation, it is best to use a control agent. The spider mite, in contrast to various louse species, has little resistance to preservatives. Particularly difficult in combating the spider mite is the size of these parasites. These are easy to miss and can then easily spread again. Therefore, the plant should be sprayed thoroughly. Tip: in the evening, spray the plant with water containing 2% yellow soap and 1% spirit. Since the eggs hatch mostly in the evening, this is particularly effective. In addition, you can increase humidity and reduce temperature. Because spider mites love a warm, dry environment.

Harmfulness to humans

For humans, spider mites are not dangerous.

Special features

At a temperature of below 12 degrees, spider mites stop evolving and go into their rest period.

SCALE LICE

Scale lice are often confused with lice. They have an eponymous flat body and are represented in various colors. Scale insects are difficult to control and can cause great damage to the plant.

Variants of the pest

There are two types of scale insects. The boisdubal schildlaus are flat, yellow lice, in which the male are smaller than the female. These are often confused with lice (lice), the lice have a rectangular body. The second species is the oleander schildlaus. These have an eponymous round shield, which, however, is not in the middle. Due to the color (white or yellow), and the shape of the 2mm pests is often compared with fried eggs.

Susceptible plants

Thyme louse occurs most often in older plants or plants with a woody stem. It is also common in orchids and all types of palm trees.

place of infestation:

Both types of scale lice occur on the underside of the leaves as well as in the trunk.

Appearance

In most cases, scale insects live in a group, which together forms a thick crust. Since the male scale insects have a waxy powder, they are often mistaken for woolly lice. Scale insects occur in different colors, including white, gray, or yellow.

Reason

Often the scale louse occurs in a dry air environment. In addition, an abundance of lime in the soil or a poorly-groomed plant may be a cause of scale insects.

Distribution

Scale insects spread through insects, birds, or the wind. In indoor plants, they spread by drafts, pets, or contact with clothes.

Damage to the plant

The insect lice attach to the plant and inject a toxic substance into the cells. This substance causes yellow, brown, or red spots on the leaves or flowers. If the pest is not fought, this leads to permanent malformation or even death of the plant.

Fighting

The louse is difficult to fight. Most of the time, there is no alternative but to use chemical means to control. If you do not want to use chemistry, you can also tap the lice with a cotton bud soaked in olive oil. The oil closes the breathing tube of the louse, and the louse will suffocate. Preventive treatment with chemical agents is effective only with repeated use. After contact with scale insects, wash and disinfect your hands carefully to avoid spreading through eggs.

Harmfulness to humans

Scale insects are not harmful to humans.

Special features

Scale lice form their shield by separating the substance itself. This shield is hard on the outside and soft on the inside. The scale insects are between 1 and 3 mm in size and lay about 100 eggs. While male scale insects only live for a maximum of 2 days, female scale insects can live up to 120 days. The scale insects are among the few species that can reproduce both sexually and asexually.

WOLLLAUS

The wolllaus belongs to the family of the louse (pseudococcidae). The name is the typical greasy hairiness of these lice. If it is not treated in time, the lice may spread to all plants.

Variants of the pest

There are several types of lice, of which the citrus louse (planococcus citri) is best known. She lives about 40 days with a heat of about 22°C. She is the only species that reproduce sexually. The louse lays in about 100 eggs, which hatch after 2 weeks.

Another common species is the long-tailed louse (pseudococcus longispinus). This louse occurs mainly in a humid environment.

Susceptible plants

Woll lice can be found on all indoor plants. However, houseplants such as the more vulnerable are the pineapple, orchid, cactus, passionflower, bromeliad, olive tree, crassula species, and the musa (banana plant) as other species.

Place of infestation

Where exactly lice attack the plant depends on the type of lice. While most lice nest directly on the plant, some species feed on the roots. The wolllaus is one of the few plagues in the world. In the summer months, the birds louse up to 100 eggs, which then hatch within 2 weeks.

Appearance

The lice have a size of 3 to 6 mm and are covered with white, floury discharge from wax wires. They use this layer to protect themselves from the elements and natural enemies. In addition, lay your eggs in this layer.

Reason

Although plants in drafts are more susceptible to woolly louse infestations, the mealybugs have no special requirements for a plant to infect them.

Distribution

Woll lice live in large groups, but they do not spread themselves, but are mostly the people responsible for the distribution over the clothes.

Damage to the plant

The mealybugs feed on phloem. This is the system that provides the plants with nutrients. The lice with their mouthparts suck the phloem out of the leaves, which causes the plant to lose waxing power. In addition, the plant can thereby get yellow or brown leaves and even must be educated. In addition, the hunts honeydew off, which is an optimal place for the formation of shimmer. As the honeydew mixes with the wool-like secretion, the leaf is completely covered. As a result, the plant receives less light, and photosynthesis becomes more difficult.

Fighting

Woll lice are cold-resistant. They can even easily survive temperatures of minus 40 degrees. For the fight, you can mix 12 grams of paraffin oil to one liter of water and spray over the lice. Alternatively, you can do this with alcohol. You must repeat this treatment thoroughly each day to be sure that the fluid has touched all lice. You can also use a pressure sprayer to simply rinse away the lice. In the case of long-term infestation, however, we recommend using chemical control.

Harmfulness to humans

Mealybugs are not harmful to humans.

Special features

Most mealybugs can reproduce both sexually and asexually.

Wool and lice

In dry room air, wool and mealybugs can spread undisturbed:

- Infestation leaves a wooly coating on the stems and leaves
- Oil-containing sprays help, for example with neem oil
- The oil stifles the lice

Black or green lice

The cause of an infestation with black or green lice is often too dry and warm location, especially places above a radiator and in the blazing sun:

- Makes visible by curling the leaves
- Especially young shoots take damage
- Formation of a sticky coating
- Wash off lice with a detergent-based solution
- Change location

Schildlaus

Similar to the other lice, too dry air promotes the spread of scale insects:

- Brown cusps on the stems and leaves
- Glued leaves that lead to crippling
- Oil-containing sprays are also used here

Healing of infested plants

To slow the spread of the pests, remove as much infected material as possible. Either cut away the infested material completely, or you try to remove the pests with a cloth. After you have come into contact with the vermin, you should disinfect your hands.

Place the plant outside or cover the floor with foils so you can "shower" it off with lukewarm water. This also works preventively. You can use a hard jet of water to simply rinse away most of the plague.

If your infested houseplant is also suitable for outdoors, you can also put it outside to prevent infection of other plants. For example, you can fight the spider mite completely. Make sure, however, that the outside temperature is high enough, and the plant is not in direct sunlight.

If you want to combat the pests with chemicals, multiple treatments are necessary. Therefore, pay close attention to the enclosed instructions for your particular product. After successful treatment, spray the plant with lukewarm rainwater to rinse off the remainder of the chemicals.

Also, clean the planter completely. Take the plant completely out of the pot and remove as much old soil as possible. In addition, check the roots of the plant for your health. Then you can refill the plant pot with new soil.

Causes

Particularly susceptible to vermin, houseplants are not properly maintained or permanently draughty. For example, if a plant has a lack of water, it can make the leaves softer, making it easier for lice to extract the juice from the plant. Of course, healthy plants can also be attacked by pests. These can often spread unnoticed by pets, other plants, or even by yourself first. Therefore, it is important to regularly check your plants for pests, paying particular attention to the lower side of the leaves. Because if you see something that does not belong there, you may be able to save the plant in time. If lice or spider mites completely attack your plant, it will be difficult for your plant.

Chapter 10

Choosing plants

There are some plants that are better for growing hydroponically. Because most people do a lot of research to find out which plants are best grown hydroponically. Here are some of the best plants that can be grown in a hydroponic system:

Tomatoes

Hydroponic hobbyists and commercial growers have a lot of interest in growing tomatoes with a hydroponic system. You will get better results if you begin your tomato plants from a small plant instead of seeds. Some disease-resistant types are Daniela and Trust. Cherry or cocktail varieties are Sweet 100s and Cherita that do best in hydroponic gardens. Heirloom varieties like Thessaloniki and Moskvich do well, too. When you grow tomatoes in a hydroponic garden, you will have to use stakes or other support systems to keep them upright. These plants need a lot of light. They have to have the right sunlight and have to be taken good care of under perfect conditions. Hot temperatures are better for this plant.

Blueberry

This is a perennial plant that is grown for its berries. They are great to grow hydroponically. You will need to use an NFT system. It would be better to use a transplant because seeds are too hard to get to grow. It does better in warmer temperatures.

Strawberries

Strawberries have been grown for many years for their fruit. They are great for a hydroponic system. It is the best plant to grow hydroponically. The NFT is the best system to grow these plants. Weather isn't a factor when growing hydroponic strawberries because it lets you harvest it all year long. They do require a lot of sun and warm temperatures.

Lotus

This water plant is also known as Nelumbo nucifera. Lotus rhizomes need to be planted in pots or tubs with gravel or sand. It needs no less than one foot of solution. Lotus is normally grown in warmer temperatures but can withstand cooler conditions.

Watercress

This is a dark leafy green that is part of the kale family. It is perfect for a hydroponic garden as it loves water. You can grow them from seeds by sowing them in pots. This aquatic plant loves water that is slightly alkaline. They need to be grown at lower temperatures. Stems from the plant can be cut off and put into new holes to begin a brand-new crop.

Chives

Chives are easily grown in hydroponic systems. It will take between six to eight weeks for them to become completely matured. They can be grown under normal conditions. Once they have matured, they can be regularly harvested. Sunlight is very important for them as they need between 12 to 14 hours each day. They need warm temperatures to thrive.

Mint

Mint plants such as spearmint and peppermint can easily be grown hydroponically. These get used as flavoring for beverages and foods for their aroma. It is best to grow these in hydroponic systems because their roots spread fast. They love warmer temperatures.

Basil

This herb is used in many culinary dishes. It can be grown easily in a hydroponic system. Purchasing some seedlings at a garden center and then transplanting them into your hydroponic garden. Make sure you rinse all the dirt off their roots before putting them into your system. They will thrive in either an NFT or a drip system. They require a lot of sunlight and need to get about 11 hours daily. They love warm temperatures.

Kale

This delicious plant is a member of the cabbage family. The best hydroponic system for this plant is the wicking system. It is easy to grow and easily taken care of. Because you are growing it inside, you don't need to worry about using pesticides. Kale can thrive in both warm and cool temperatures.

Lettuce

This is a member of the daisy family and it is an annual plant. This is normally the best choice for beginner hydroponic gardeners. It is super easy to grow because they grow really fast in a hydroponic system. You can harvest these constantly once they reach maturity. You will always have a supply of fresh lettuce. You can use either the Ebb and Flow, aeroponic, or NFT system. It can be grown in cooler temperatures.

Spinach

Begin the spinach seeds by growing them in rockwool. Put the seeds in drilled holes and then hang just above the nutrient solution. An Ebb and Flow system is best for this. Plants that are germinating need to be raised just a bit to allow oxygen to reach their roots because rockwool isn't a great conductor. Once the seeds have sprouted, you can move them to a permanent place. You need to allow about 20 square inches for each plant. This leafy green is another good plant to grow in a hydroponic system. This plant does better when it has its roots submerged in a nutrient solution that is about five inches deep. Because it can thrive in cooler temperatures, it doesn't need as much light. You can constantly harvest this plant for 12 weeks if you have the right climate and conditions.

Radishes

Radishes are another easy vegetable to grow hydroponically. You can start these from seeds, and you should see some seedlings between three and seven days. They love cooler temperatures and don't need much light.

Cucumbers

This is a common vining plant that can be grown in either a normal hydroponic system or a commercial greenhouse. They grow very fast under the right conditions and will give extremely high yields. There are many sizes and types of cucumbers that will all grow very well in a hydroponic system. These are warm plants so they will need warmer temperatures to thrive.

Beans

Beans are very low maintenance but very productive. They can be easily grown hydroponically. Lima beans, pinto beans, pole beans, and green beans can all be grown hydroponically. You are going to need a trellis or something for the vines to grow upon. Germinating seeds will take between three and eight days. You can begin harvesting beans usually after six weeks. The crop will continue to produce for about four months.

Peppers

Peppers will need the same growing conditions that tomatoes need. They need a large amount of light along with warm temperatures. Peppers will take between two and three months to get to maturity. You can grow them from either seeds or small plants from your local garden supply store. You will need to stake these just like tomatoes. The best varieties that thrive in a hydroponic garden are Fellini, Nairobi, cubico, mazurka, gold flame, habanero, jalapeno, and cayenne.

Peas

Snow peas like cooler temperatures in the fall and spring. They can't handle the hot summer sun. If temperatures get over 86 degrees Fahrenheit, it will cause a poor pod set. Before you plant, you are going to need to choose the type of peas you are going to plant snap, snow, or English. The English variety only produces seeds that are edible. You can eat both the pod and seed of the snap and snow peas. Peas will be ready to harvest about three weeks after you see flowers.

Eggplant

Eggplants need to be planted in full sunlight. Plants can become injured by frost and don't do well when exposed to the cold for long periods of time. Eggplants need to be treated like tomatoes. The main difference is eggplants like the temp to be a bit warmer. Start them in nursery stock in the early part of spring. Allow between 60 and 100 days to get to maturity.

Cauliflower

This belongs to the same family as collards, cabbage, kale, and broccoli. It will have a compact head that is on average about six inches. It is made of undeveloped flower buds. These flowers are attached to one main center stalk. Having a sturdy support system is necessary to keep everything but the roots out of the solution. You can do this by using a layer of gravel where the roots ca still reaches the solution or using a netting that lets the roots grow through it. The nutrient solution can be delivered by a drip system two times daily. This keeps the roots from getting too moist. This is a very cost-effective vegetable since it loves lower temperatures and doesn't need to be constantly provided with solution.

Cabbage

You will need to buy cabbage seedling to grow in rockwool cubes. Once they have grown big enough to stand alone, you can put them in hydroponic pots and place the cube in growing medium. Cabbage plants need about two feet between each one for a growing room.

Broccoli

Broccoli has a large head that is normally green. The "flowering heads" are arranged as branches that sprout out of a thick edible stalk. The head is surrounded by leaves just like cabbage. Most varieties are perennial. You can plant this in May and harvest it in the winter or early spring of the next year. It is a heavy plant that will need to be staked.

Thyme

This is a member of the mint family and has been valued as a very sweet herb. It will have small pink or lavender flowers and is normally grown as an ornamental, border plant, or an herb to be eaten. Thyme needs to be planted early in spring. It is a hardy plant and grows in most conditions. It likes full sun and only a small amount of fertilization.

Tarragon

This is a perennial herb that is used for seasoning things like vinegar. Tarragon can grow to about three feet tall and like the moderate sun. It likes to have some shared during the hot part of the day. Tarragon doesn't have a lot of fragrance while it is growing but once the tops are harvested, the oil will begin emitting their sweet smell.

Sage

This is a shrub that is grown for dressings, seasonings, to season meats, and to flavor cheese and sausages. It can be grown from seeds. It needs to be protected from the cold and thrives in full sun. Since the plants can grow three feet in diameter, they need to be grown no less than four feet apart. Sage leaves need to be harvested before it blooms and then dried on screens in a well-ventilated room or in a dehydrator. You can then store it in an airtight container.

Rosemary

This is a hardy evergreen shrub that is grown for its leaves that are used as a seasoning and produces an oil that can be used in medicines. It will bear light blue flowers in April or May. The foliage will be wooly and white on the bottom and shiny and dark on top. Plants could grow to be six feet tall and last for many years, but they need to be protected from the cold. They like full sun and alkaline soil but will tolerate some moderate shade.

Parsley

This is a great herb to grow hydroponically. It has a very long taproot so the container you put it in needs to be at least 12 inches deep.

Oregano

This is a hardy perennial that could grow up to two feet tall. It will have a white or pink flower. Oregano can be grown from seeds or the main plant divided. You can stimulate the foliage by cutting the flowers back. You can replant once the plants get woody. This will take about four years. You can use the leaves when picked or dry them for later use. Oregano can be used to flavor pizzas, spaghetti sauce, or other Italian dishes.

Marjoram

This is a perennial herb that is grown for its flavor. It has been used to flavor meat dishes and dressings. It loves full sun. Because the seeds are extremely small, it is best to grow in flats inside a greenhouse and once they sprout, you can transplant them once frost has passed.

Lavender

This is the common name for most fragrant shrubs or herbs. It has been grown as a decorative plant and for its wonderful scent. The dried flowers can be put into sachets to perfume linens or clothing. The green parts can be used to make lavender water, aromatic vinegar, and "oil of spike." Real lavender isn't hard in northern gardens. It is normally found in the mild weather on the Pacific Coast and the South.

Fennel

This is a perennial plant that will grow to about four feet tall. Their leaves are divided into thread-like segments are a light green in color and look a lot like dill. It can grow from seeds that were planted in spring and will grow best when in full sun. Plants will need to be staked once they reach 18 inches. Harvest when the seeds once they ripen. The flower stalks are great to eat right before they blossom. Fennel seeds can be used as a condiment. The leaves taste a lot like anise. Stems can be eaten just like celery. The seeds can be used in vegetable dishes and cheese spreads.

Dill

Dill is a great addition to any hydroponic garden. It grows more once it is harvested. If you replace spent plants with new ones about every three or four weeks will keep you in a constant supply of dill. The compact variety will produce an abundant lush of growth that will give you a lot of cuttings from one plant.

Coriander / Cilantro

Cilantro looks a lot like parsley. If it is grown for its leaves, it is considered cilantro but if it is allowed to seed, it is called coriander. Coriander needs cooler temperatures. It will grow best in full sun.

Chervil

This is a plant that likes cooler temperatures and not a lot of sunlight. Cooler roots are necessary to make sure that it grows well. If you don't provide the plant with shade and a way to keep it cool, this plant is hard to grow in the summer. It is ready to harvest in about four weeks. This is the perfect winter crop.

Chamomile

This grows great in soilless culture. You can use it to make chamomile tea and has many medicinal qualities. It loves full sun but will tolerate shady conditions.

Catnip

This grows well in a hydroponic garden either in partial shade or full sun. It is perennial and a member of the mint family. It will grow to about five feet tall. It can easily be grown from seed, stem cuttings, or dividing the root ball. Seeds need to be sown in late fall or early spring.

Anise

This is a feathery annual that will grow to about two feet tall. It has finely cut serrated leaves and small, white flowers. The seeds and the leaves can be used and they both have a sweet taste that is similar to licorice. It will grow fairly fast from seeds and needs to be planted after frost has passed. The leaves can be cut when the plant is large enough. The seeds could be gathered one month after the flowers have bloomed. Anise leaves can be put into salads or used as a garnish. The seeds can flavor confections like cookies and cakes.

Flowers

Growing flowers in a hydroponic garden creates a beautiful scene. They can be grown in huge numbers and you can grow them all year long. Most flowers do great in hydroponic gardens. Once the seedlings are large enough, the flowers could be transplanted or cut.

Chapter 11

Tips and tricks to growing healthy herbs, vegetables and fruits

Growing plants on the walls of moss

The legendary Babylonian queen Semiramis left a descendant of the seventh wonder of the world - the fabulous "hanging gardens". Today, every amateur flower grower can successfully compete with Semiramis. However, to successfully compete with Semiramis, he must know how to build vertical (in the literal sense of the word) beds. This opportunity is given by the plant culture on the walls of moss.

Walls of moss, possibly the most original way to grow plants without soil, is a variation of the method known widely in the Republic of South Africa under the name and is widely used in this country. According to this method, these plants are grown not in a purely nutrient solution or on an inorganic substrate, but in an organic filler, that is, on suitably prepared plant materials, periodically moistened with a nutrient solution. From South Africa, information about this method reached Switzerland, and here, the method was picked up and developed with great imagination with many successful options by several people. With the help of some simple base (frame), the old horizontal bed is turned into a vertical one.

This creates an ideal opportunity for the best use of space to accommodate the cultivated area.

The first attempts to grow useful plants on vertical beds were made in 1941, during difficult times. They wanted to know if it would be possible to grow more fresh vegetables using this method. Basically, all the experiments gave a positive result, and nevertheless, despite these promising results, the culture of plants on the walls of moss until today has not found recognition in industrial vegetable growing, but it has found a greater response to amateur gardeners. An attentive observer every year sees more and more flower walls glistening with colorful paints in gardens, on terraces, balconies, flat roofs, etc. And this is not surprising...

The basis

Before we start tinkering with something, we should outline the basic principles of the method in a few words.

The thing is to firmly hold, using a suitable base, in a vertical position a moisture-absorbing organic substrate, which should simultaneously serve as a source of nutrient solution and a medium for the growth of plant roots. The filler in the finished base, or substrate, is periodically moistened with the prepared nutrient solution. Planting or sowing seeds is carried out through the holes in the base on all available vertical and horizontal surfaces.

Common in some places, the so-called strawberry barrel is the simplest suitable base. Any barrel that is unsuitable for anything else is suitable here unless it has been used before to store materials harmful to plants (chemicals, paints, etc.). In the walls of the barrel, drill holes with a diameter of 4 - 5 cm at a distance of 15 - 20 cm from one another. Only at the bottom of the barrel do they leave a belt of 15 - 20 cm wide intact. Before filling the barrel with a substrate, a small hole is drilled in its bottom through which excess liquid can flow. For the same purpose, large gravel is used, laid on the bottom of the barrel with a layer 1 cm high.

Now stock up on an empty tin can and a bunch of brushwood or a bunch of twigs. We put the jar (it should be 15–20 cm high) in the middle of the gravel layer and vertically set up a bunch of brushwood or twigs, and fill the rest of the barrel space to the top with a substrate.

Barrels prepared in this way are planted mainly with strawberries, which preserve decorative qualities throughout the growing season and, in addition, continuously produce fruit.

The substrate is poured with a nutrient solution from above, using a watering can, and the brushwood in the center of the barrel ensures a quick and even distribution of the liquid. Finally, a small bar is nailed at an angle above each hole to drain rainwater flowing down from above. The finished barrel can also be painted with oil paint, choosing a color to your liking. After painting, the barrel is completely ready.

Vertical hydroponics

We now turn to the form that is probably used most often, namely the wall. The materials necessary for the construction of the first small experimental walls can be collected without much labor and almost without cost, especially if you delve into your own pantry. Metal rods, planks, slats, trim boards, a few nails and a bit of wire, and maybe the old wire mesh, you can probably find anytime, anywhere.

A prudent amateur will, first of all, think about the pre-treatment of building material. It is highly advisable to impregnate lumber with a substance that protects them well from moisture in order to protect them from rapid destruction. It is strongly recommended that you carefully paint over all metal parts (nets, wire, rods) with ordinary bitumen paint. This is done not only to protect against rust but also because, as it turned out, metal parts not coated with paint can react with a nutrient solution, as a result of which substances very toxic to plants can pass into the solution. This, of course, must be prevented. Therefore, you should choose only such means of impregnation and insulation, which certainly do not contain plant poisons (paints, which include the so-called heavy metals, are extremely toxic).

If the proposed structure, for example, for the garden is stationary, then four poles are simply driven into the ground in the right place and, you set them at the same height, connected for greater stability with rails of the appropriate thickness. Then the foundation is ready.

If it is planned to put a flower wall on a terrace, in a garden or elsewhere, then, of course, the portable base must meet these requirements. Therefore, we first build a solid base in the form of a wall about 50 cm long, 50 cm high, and 30 cm wide.

With such dimensions, a wall completely planted with plants will weigh about 65 kg and can still be carried.

As a next step, we will take care of limiting the side surfaces, and here you can go in different ways. It is very advisable to make a crate of vertical narrow rails with a distance between them of 5 - 7 cm. In this case, with the usually observed subsidence of the substrate mass, plants already planted between the planks will not be damaged. Since the mass of the substrate moistened with the nutrient solution is heavy, it accordingly exerts considerable pressure on the side rails. In order to prevent the strips from bulging out on more or less high walls, a reinforcing horizontal bar should be strengthened every 40 to 50 cm on the side surfaces, which, in addition, is connected by a wire to a similar bar on the opposite wall of the base. If this is done, then you need not worry about the side surfaces.

Another, often chosen and leading to the same goal is the use of wire mesh. Any nets with mesh sizes from 50 to a maximum of 75 mm are suitable for this if they are coated with an insulating layer of bitumen paint. The advantage of nets is that after a short time they become invisible to the eye since a thin wire is immersed in the mass of the substrate or masked by plants. The disadvantage of the grid is that when the mass of the substrate settles, the plants in individual cells are suspended on the grid and are damaged.

However, this can be avoided with a sufficiently careful filling of the mesh with a substrate. Lateral swellings are especially easy to form on wire meshes, so you need to take care of suitable screeds.

Hydroponic "life hacks"

Separate barrels or walls are planted with plants from above or from all sides. By this, however, the choice of forms is by no means exhausted. You can easily build planted columns, half columns, cubes, as well as arbitrary shapes like trellises, pyramids, garlands, hanging curtain rods and pots, etc. There is no need to dwell on the manufacture of the basis for all of these forms. Therefore, we confine ourselves to only general provisions for all forms.

When choosing a shape and determining the size of the frame, you can more closely follow personal tastes and adapt to the particularities of the place. However, it is always necessary to reckon with the following: plants must have a sufficient volume of substrate for the roots and have a stock of the solution corresponding to their size and number. The height and length of the structure can be chosen completely arbitrarily, but the width (thickness of the substrate layer) must have the following minimum dimensions: when planting with plants on all sides - at least 30 cm; when planting with plants on one side - at least 18 cm.

If this condition is met, you can be sure that the supply of nutrient solution to the plants is enough for 8 to 10 days.

We have already seen that vertical beds or walls can be stationary or mobile. They can even be put on wheels. In order to use the terrace as a flowering screen in accordance with the position of the sun, an enterprising gardener built several metal frames that could be made together like building blocks and made of the large floral walls. When decorating the stage, stands, and assembly halls, they always successfully replace the slightly treasured greenery of palm trees and evergreen shrubs.

Various vertical walls can also be used to decorate walls and parts of buildings. They can be suspended at any height, and the rear surface adjacent to the walls of the building can be impermeable to moisture (for example, from tin coated with an insulating layer, or from the roofing material, roofing felt, or plastic film) so that the walls of the building do not suffer. It is very advisable to put a couple of bars between the back surface of the base and the wall of the building, which will provide better ventilation.

Here, by the way, it should be noted that it is already possible to obtain bases made industrially from asbestos cement or metal. Since they are in good shape and made very reasonably, they certainly deserve attention.

Gardening tricks

A wall of moss or peat can also be used for internal gardening. However, in this case, it is necessary to provide some kind of receiver to drain a possible excess of nutrient solution. The receiver can be a painted tin can or even a plastic tub installed under the base or suspended from it. With a known dexterity, you should immediately make a device for draining the liquid - it can be a faucet or just a siphon tube. If all this is provided for, we can be calm for the completely modern conditions for indoor plants that have been created.

Here, in fact, all the most important guidelines that must be observed when building the foundations for growing plants on a substrate of moss or peat. It should only be recalled that when planting young plants, you need to take into account the space required for a fully developed plant. For example, if a fully planted foundation should ultimately have a length of 2 m, then a 2.6 m long frame is sufficient because the height of the plant on the end surfaces will be at least 0.2 m. In conclusion, another indication for the site owner demanding on himself familiar with the craft of a bricklayer: a flower wall can be folded out of brick, or better yet, of uncut stone. To do this, first lay the foundation with a width of about 60 cm and the desired length. The top of the foundation is leveled and a groove is made in it to drain excess fluid with an inclination to one side.

There is no need for the whole process of work, you should only warn that cement should not be saved. The strength of the structure will increase significantly if you use a solution with a narrow ratio of sand to cement (2: 1 or 3: 1). When the masonry is finished, you need to hold the brush and cover the inner surface of the masonry and the top of the cement, i.e. all surfaces that will come in contact with the substrate, bitumen paint, to prevent the influence of lime or bricks on the nutrient solution.

A layer of coarse quartz sand with a thickness of 5-8 cm is first poured into the finished base. It will ensure the rapid removal of excess moisture. Then the substrate is stuffed, which should be very moistened to speed up the process of natural subsidence. After this, you can start planting the plants.

Another important point! You can greatly facilitate your work if at the beginning of the masonry, at the end of the wall above the lower end of the gutter, several stones or bricks are fixed so that they can be easily removed. Then, using the poker, you can easily dig out the substrate from the usually inaccessible narrow space. Another detail: curly seams made of white cement give a special decorative effect to a wall made of bright red facing brick.

Using this method, you save the most space and get the most yield from your hydroponic garden!

Chapter 12

In full bloom: secrets to growing hydroponics herbs and vegetables successfully

After building your hydroponics garden, you are most likely just raring to go and grow your herbs and vegetables. But you do have to realize that as easy as growing your plants hydroponically might be, there are a number of things that you need to know to become successful at it.

Plant nutrients

In truth, much of the work involved in gardening with soil is done by nature. This is because the nutrients that plants need to grow can be found in most types of soils. But when you grow your plants in a hydroponics garden, which does not use any soil at all, what you are basically doing is taking charge of nature's work yourself.

1. Growing your herbs and vegetables hydroponically lets you enhance the quality of the nutrients that you feed them with. The most common way of doing this is by making your own nutrient solution at home with the help of fertilizer salts. You can actually buy the fertilizer salts in bulk from chemical suppliers, gardening stores, nurseries, plant food suppliers, and agricultural suppliers.

2. You will find that some types of fertilizer salts are the most ideal to use in hydroponics gardening. Although you can always just take your pick from other similar types of fertilizer salts, the former have several properties (more stability, better solubility, longer shelf life, and lower cost) that make them the more excellent choice).

• Potassium chloride: Instead of using potassium sulphate, you can use potassium chloride to provide your hydroponics plants the key nutrient potassium they require for proper growth. You have to keep in mind, however, that you might have to avoid using potassium chloride beyond a few days. Otherwise, its chlorine component might cause harm to your herbs and vegetables, especially if the water you are using in your hydroponics system has been treated with chlorine beforehand.

• Magnesium nitrate: You can use either magnesium nitrate or magnesium sulphate to supply your hydroponics plants' need for magnesium, but the latter is the cheaper and more accessible option (think Epsom salts).

• Ferric citrate: Ferrous sulphate can be used even if you simply dissolve it in cold water. Meanwhile, you will need to use hot water in order to dissolve ferrous citrate.

3. All kinds of plants, whether you grow them in soil or hydroponically, require three key elements in order to grow properly, namely nitrogen, phosphorus, and potassium (N, P, K).

• Nitrogen: This essential element is responsible for allowing your hydroponics herbs and vegetables to produce leaves as well as grow stems. Plants also need nitrogen for cell building.

• Phosphorus: Phosphorus is an essential element that plays a key role in your hydroponics plants' ability to grow healthy roots.

• Potassium: Your hydroponics herbs and vegetables also need potassium in order to effectively absorb the energy produced by their photosynthetic activities.

4. Your hydroponics plants will also need the following trace elements for proper growth: Sulphur (for producing your plants' energy and for supporting the role of phosphorus); iron (for aiding in chlorophyll production); manganese (for supporting nitrogen absorption; zinc (for the conversion of energy); copper (for chlorophyll production); magnesium (for the effective distribution of phosphorus) in your plants; calcium (for encouraging the growth of roots and the absorption of potassium by your plants; chlorine (for photosynthetic activities); and molybdenum (for assisting in various chemical reactions).

5. It would be best for you to strictly follow the general guidelines regarding the use of fertilizer salts and to save the ratio experimentations for later.

Ph testing

pH testing is extremely important in ensuring the success of your hydroponics gardening. You need to keep the pH of your nutrient solution in the right range so that all the nutrients are carried to and absorbed by your herbs and vegetables.

1. It is easy to control your nutrient solution's pH: Simply get yourself a dip strip or a test kit (you can get one that is similar to that used in swimming pools). Both the strip and the kit don't cost that much and are not too difficult to learn.

Know that there really is no need for you to purchase a costly electronic pH meter. Another important thing to keep in mind is that the ideal pH of a hydroponics system's nutrient solution is 6.0, and that 5.5 to 6.5 is the proper pH range.

2. Test your nutrient solution's pH whenever you are mixing a fresh batch. It is best to allow the newly mixed nutrient solution to settle for a few hours before performing an initial pH test. After one hour, you may then perform the pH test again. You might also consider testing the pH of your nutrient solution twice a week or even daily.

3. Adjusting the pH of your nutrient solution calls for strictly following the directions indicated on your purchased pH adjuster kit. Know that a tiny amount is extremely potent, which is why you should do this carefully.

In case your pH adjuster kit solution runs out, you could try fixing your nutrient solution's pH by using white vinegar and baking soda. The white vinegar can be used to lower the pH while the baking soda can be used to raise it. Keep in mind, however, that this is another spot-fix solution and should not be performed on a frequent basis. Both the white vinegar and baking soda are unstable and un-buffered substances.

Growing healthy herbs and vegetables

Keeping your hydroponics herbs and vegetables healthy, strong, and more pest- and disease-resistant is easy if you know how to keep your hydroponics system healthy as well. All you need to do is to make sure that your system is operating in proper growing conditions. Try these helpful tips on how to do it:

1. Make sure that the humidity in your hydroponics system is kept low (if possible, 50 to 60 percent) and the temperature is kept cool (75 degrees is most preferable).

2. Ensure proper air circulation and ventilation in your hydroponics system to keep mold and fungi at bay.

3. Do not do the following:

• Overwatering: This will make your growing medium soggy enough to allow the growth of algae, mildew, and mold.

• Doing indoor work last: It is best to do your outside gardening after you are done with your indoor work. Also, avoid visiting your hydroponics garden immediately after having gone to a nursery.

• Bringing in outside visitors: Keep yourself from making the most of your artificial lights by bringing soil-planted specimens or houseplants into your hydroponics herbs' and vegetables' grow space.

• Puff on a cigarette: Avoid smoking inside your grow space. If you have to smoke, do it outside, and make sure to thoroughly wash your hands with water and soap before handling your hydroponics herbs and vegetables.

Cleanliness and sanitation

Cleanliness and sanitation are the expert hydroponics gardener's well-kept secrets to growing their herbs and vegetables successfully. Here are some easy tips to follow:

1. Make sure to get rid of every dead leaf and plant debris you find in your grow space.

2. To prevent any pests from thriving on decomposing plant matter and to keep diseases at bay, keep your grow space free from nutrient solution spills and scattered growing media. You should also take any dying or dead plant out of your hydroponics garden and throw it outside.

3. Set aside your pruners, trowel, and other gardening tools that you will specifically use in your hydroponics garden. Make sure that these tools are kept in the grow space. You should also see to it that they are not used on any outside plants or houseplants.

4. It would be best to disinfect all your hydroponics gardening tools frequently in a water/bleach solution (10%) or in isopropyl alcohol.

5. Bring all of your old herbs and vegetables outside your grow room. You can either allow them to decompose in a composting bin or just throw them into the trash bin. If you happen to have any remaining nutrient solution from a batch

you have mixed, use them on your shrubs and trees out in the yard.

6. Set aside an entire weekday afternoon to thoroughly disinfect your entire hydroponics garden. Carefully break down the components of your hydroponics system before taking them outside. Use a gentle brush and mild dishwashing liquid to give them all a good scrub. After rinsing all the scrubbed components well, flush the whole hydroponics system in a solution of water and bleach (90 percent water and 10 percent bleach). Allow the system to stand for thirty minutes before flushing again, this time more thoroughly and using clean water.

7. As a final touch, use a bleach disinfectant in wiping down the walls and floors of your grow space.

Pest control

It would be unrealistic to say that you can completely protect your hydroponics garden from pests. Any type of garden would naturally attract pests at some point, during which they can damage the plants. Making sure that pests are prevented from entering your garden in the first place is the most effective way of fending them off.

1. Consider starting your hydroponics herbs and vegetables from seedlings. This will significantly reduce any risk of your plants developing a number of problems with pests. Buying mature herbs and vegetables from garden centers welcomes the possibility of bringing pests into your home, since chances

are high that the soil in which the plants are grown already have pests lurking in them.

2. Prevent any pests from invading your hydroponics garden by considering the idea of growing your own herbs and vegetables seedlings through germination. This way, you also gain a wonderful learning experience that you can share to your kids.

3. Take the time to monitor your hydroponics garden every day. Doing so will help you catch any pests that might find their way onto your garden, before they cause an infestation. It helps to check out any leaf holes, leaf discoloration, and other signs of plant damage due to pests.

4. Make sure to use only containers and system components that have been thoroughly cleansed and sanitized. This is an effective way of keeping your hydroponics garden from turning into a breeding ground for pests such as insects.

5. It is extremely important that any dead leaves are removed from your herbs or vegetables. You should also see to it that you isolate any plant that you think may be showing signs of infection.

6. You should also make sure that adequate air flow and other proper growing conditions are maintained within your hydroponics garden at all times.

7. Watch out for any of the following common pests that might cause trouble in your hydroponics garden:

•   Aphids: You might think that aphids are those teeny green critters you usually see in your garden. The fact is, aphids come in colors other than green, so be sure to check the underside of your herbs' and vegetables' leaves for any clusters of aphids.

•   Mealy bugs: Mealy bugs are those harmless-looking, fluffy, white, and cotton-like bugs you can usually find on the stems or undersides of the leaves of your plants.

•   Scale: Another type of pest that can usually be found hiding on your plants' leaves (undersides) is this small, brown insect.

•   Spider mites: You may have to use a magnifying glass to check your plants for any spider mites, whose usual signs of damage to plants are the discoloration of leaves.

•   White flies: See if your herbs and vegetables show any signs of a black film that appears similar to mold buildup – that is usually an indication of the presence of white flies.

8. As mentioned earlier, you may experience pest infestation on your hydroponics plants at some point. But there are means by which you can eliminate the pests and preserve your herbs and vegetables:

•   Get rid of pests naturally by introducing ladybugs and other beneficial insects to your hydroponics garden. These types of insects are able to fight off aphid infestation by eating the said aphids.

- Neem oil is a derivative of the neem plant and has been shown to be effective in destroying pests. Neem oil does this by keeping the insects from laying any eggs.

- Organic pest sprays, whether made on your own or purchased at the store, is also effective in fighting off pests in your hydroponics garden. These sprays, usually made with a solution of water and soap, and then blended with citrus, are simply sprayed over your plants' leaves in order to kill the pests.

Chapter 13

Light and monitoring equipment

Lights

NATURAL LIGHTS

This chapter is going to cover the basics of lighting for your hydroponic system. Of course, you can use natural lighting, placing your outdoor hydroponics system on the south side of your house, but in this chapter, I want to cover artificial lighting.

One of the most important things you need to learn about when you are learning about growing with hydroponics, besides the actual system, is the lighting.

If your plants do not receive the light they need, they are not going to grow properly nor are they going to produce the amount of fruit you want. To become the best grower, you always want to find out what is limiting you the most. Learning what is limiting you the most and learning as much about it as you can is going to allow you to increase the growth of your plants without adjusting anything else.

When you think about lighting, you have to realize that no matter how great your system is, no matter how great the medium you are using is, no matter how high the quality of your fertilizer, without the proper light, your plants will never be able to grow healthy, strong plants.

The first thing you have to know about is the color of light that your bulbs produce. You see, every bulb will produce a colored light that is measured in degrees Kelvin; this is how the hue produced by the bulb is specified.

Most plants are going to grow better with a bulb that is 6500° degrees Kelvin. Flowering plants, on the other hand, are going to grow better at 2700k degrees Kelvin.

Of course, there are many different variables that will affect the rate at which your plants grow, but the most important of these variables is light. Using a high quality light is the only way you can guarantee your plants will grow to their fullest potential.

ARTIFICIAL LIGHTS

There are a number of lighting systems on the market today and each of these systems have their own pro's and con's that need to be taken into consideration, but it is important for you to remember that choosing the correct lighting for your indoor growing is the most important thing you can do to ensure effective growing.

Incandescent lamps are the first of the lighting systems that I want to talk about. These are what are known as the standard household light bulbs, and they are not very efficient when it comes to growing plants. They actually only have about a 5% efficiency rate. Incandescent lamps are not recommended for growing plants.

Fluorescent lights are a great choice if you are planning on growing your plants indoors. The best fluorescent lights are high output lights, which are about 7 times more efficient. This simply means that the lights will put out more light while using less electricity. A wide range of spectrums are available when it comes to fluorescent lamps and the 6500k are the best for indoor growing.

If you are growing larger plants, using fluorescent lighting is not advised as these are better for smaller plants. The fluorescent lamps are not as good at penetrating as the high intensity discharge lamps are.

There are many options for growing plants when it comes to fluorescent lights. You can choose lights that will be hung above the plants or that are hung to the side of the plants.

Another very popular form of fluorescent lights are the compact fluorescent lights or CFLs. These were designed as an alternative to the normal household bulbs or incandescent lights because they use less electricity and are supposed to have a longer life than incandescent bulbs. The CFL's are good for growers who are on a small budget and are growing small plants.

The great thing about CFLs is that you do not have to worry about the wiring, they don't require anything more than a standard socket, and they are extremely low in price. If you are going to use CFLs, you should consider using a reflector of some type, otherwise you will be wasting a lot of light that you could be using for your plants.

High intensity discharge lamps are the next type of lighting that I want to talk to you about. Also known as HID, these bulbs are the top pick for most growers. These are usually the types are generally used in street lights, parking lots, and warehouses. These lights are the top pick for today's growers because their output is 8 times more efficient than regular household light bulbs.

Light emitting diodes or LEDs are some of the new technology that growers are using for their plants because they use much less electricity than the other light sources mentioned.

There are many different things you need to think about when you are choosing your lighting. Your budget is the first thing that you need to think about when you are choosing your lighting for your hydroponics system. Those who are working with a low budget will be better off using T5 fluorescent tubes as will small scale growers.

If you have a large budget, the HID lamps are the highest quality, but you will need to consider getting them their own ventilation system because they will significantly raise the temperature of the room otherwise.

LED lights are great for those who are going to be growing for a long period of time because they will save you a ton of money on your electric bill. For example, some growers save as much as $5,000 over the lifetime of their LED bulbs.

Of course, this is just an example and it all depends on the price of electricity, how much you are willing to invest upfront, how often you use the lights, the type of environment the lighting system will be in, and so forth.

Once you have chosen your hydroponics system and your medium, you will need to spend some time thinking about the type of lighting system you will be using. It is important to remember that the lighting system is the most important factor when it comes to growing your plants indoors and it is not something you should take lightly.

Monitoring equipment

pH meter

pH is a measure of how acidic or how alkaline water is. A pH of 7 is neutral. pH levels that range from 1 to 6 are acidic, and levels from 8 to 14 are considered alkaline or basic.

Different plants have their preferences regarding pH levels. To ensure the best possible growth, you need to have a way of testing and then adjusting the pH level of your water.

For example:

Cabbage likes pH levels of 7.5

Tomatoes like a pH of 6-6.5

Sweet potatoes like a pH of 5.2-6

Peppers like a pH of 5.5-7

Lettuce and broccoli like a pH of 6-7

We will talk about why balancing pH is essential later in the book.

A pH meter can be obtained from local hydroponics stores or online. You need to calibrate the sensor with the calibration powder that comes with the meter. A basic pH meter will cost you $10 to $20.

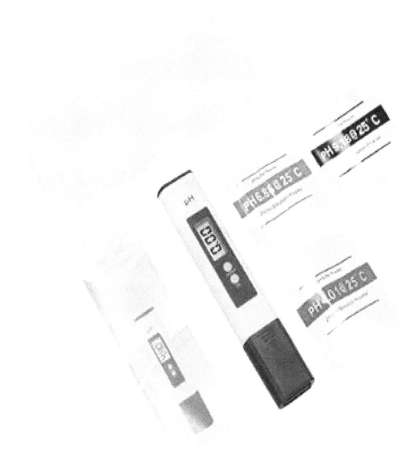

A basic pH meter

Don't use paper test strips for the water because they are inaccurate. Most of the time, a pH meter is offered in combination with a TDS or EC meter, which we will talk about next.

EC meter

Electrical conductivity is a measurement of how easily electricity passes through the water, the higher the ion content, the better it is at conducting electricity.

All water has ions in it. When you add nutrients to the water, you are increasing the ion content, effectively increasing the electrical conductivity.

EC or Electrical Conductivity is an integral part of the hydroponics equation. The simplest way of explaining this is as a guide to salts dissolved in water. Its unit is siemens per meter, but in hydroponics, we use millisiemens per meter.

In short, the higher the number of salts in the water, the higher the conductivity. Water that has no salt (distilled water) will have zero conductivity.

Lettuce likes an EC of 1.2 (or 1.2 millisiemens), while basil likes an EC of 2.

A $15 TDS & EC meter from amazon

That is why it is so important to know your EC and what your plants prefer, it will help you to ensure your system is at the right level.

However, electrical conductivity needs are also affected by the weather. When it is hot, the plants evaporate more water. That is why you need to decrease the EC in hot summer months. In colder winter months, you need to increase the EC.

In warm weather, you need to decrease the EC.

In cold weather, you need to increase the EC.

An EC meter doesn't tell you the specific amount of which mineral or fertilizer is in the water. If you only use a nutrient solution using the right ratios, you shouldn't worry.

Just because it doesn't monitor individual nutrients, doesn't mean it's not useful. Salt levels that are too high will damage your plants.

You generally need to keep them between 0.8 and 1.2 for leafy greens and between 2 and 3.5 for fruiting crops like tomatoes. The source of the water can influence the EC reading. More on this later.

Sometimes, you see the recommended nutrient levels listed as CF. CF is the conductivity factor. This is like EC, used in Europe. If you multiply EC by ten, you will become CF.

For example, lettuce grows best in an EC of 0.8 to 1.2. This is a CF of 8 to 12.

TDS meter

TDS stands for total dissolved salts. You may hear some hydroponics growers referring to the TDS and not EC. These are both used to determine the strength of your hydroponic solution. If you buy a TDS meter, there will also be an option to switch to EC readings.

It is crucial to understand that TDS is a calculated figure. TDS readings are converted from an EC reading. The problem occurs when you don't know which calculation method was used to produce the TDS; there are several different ones.

In general, EC and CF readings are used in Europe, while TDS is an American measurement. But, regardless of which measurement you choose to use, they are both effectively the same thing: a measure of the nutrient levels in your solution.

The NaCI Conversion factor

This is effectively measuring salt in the water. The conversion factor for this mineral is your micro siemens figure multiplied by any number between 0.47 and 0.5. You'll find most TDS meters use 0.5. This is the easiest one for you to remember and calculate. Most of the meters sold will use the NaCl conversion factor.

As an example, if you have a reading of 1 EC (1 milli Siemens or 1000 micro Siemens), you will have a TDS reading of 500ppm.

```
1000 micro Siemens x 0.5 = 500ppm
```

Natural Water Conversion factor

This conversion factor is referred to as the 4-4-2; this quantifies its contents. Forty percent sodium sulfate, forty percent sodium bicarbonate, and twenty percent sodium chloride.

Again, the conversion factor is a range, this time between 0.65 and 0.85. Most TDS meters will use 0.7.

For example, 1 EC (1000 micro Siemens) will be 700 ppm with a TDS meter that uses the natural water conversion.

```
1000 micro Siemens x 0.7 = 700ppm
```

Potassium Chloride, KCI Conversion factor

This conversion factor is not a range this time. It is simply a figure of 0.55. Your EC meter reading 1EC or 1000 micro Siemens will equate to 550 ppm.

```
1000 micro Siemens x 0.55 = 550ppm
```

These are not all the possible conversion options, but they are the most common. The first, NaCl is the most used today.

Dissolved oxygen sensor

Plant roots need oxygen to remain healthy and ensure the plant grows properly. The dissolved oxygen sensor will help you to understand how much oxygen is available in the water and ensure it's enough to keep your plants healthy.

If plants don't get enough oxygen to their roots, they can die. A minimum of 5 ppm is recommended.

A dissolved oxygen meter will be expensive for the hobbyist to buy, especially when you are starting. That is why dissolved oxygen meters are generally not purchased by people who do hydroponics for fun. A good meter can cost you $170 to $500 for a reputable brand.

You do not need to invest in one if you oxygenate the water. Oxygenation of the water can be done by using an air pump with an airstone in the water tank. Depending on the method of growing, you don't need to aerate the water.

The dissolved oxygen in the water will be at its lowest during the summer. The water heats up, and the dissolved oxygen becomes less available. While your plants can do very well in winter, they might lack oxygen during summer.

Net Pots

In some systems, you are going to need net pots to hold the plants. This is mostly true for deep water culture (DWC), Kratky, wick systems, Aeroponics, fogponics, dutch buckets, and possibly vertical towers.

Make sure you get the net pots with a lip on top to keep them from falling through. The standard size for lettuce is two inches (five centimeters). If you want to use tomatoes with dutch buckets, six inches (fifteen centimeters) is recommended.

3 and 2-inch (7 and 5 cm) net pots

If you are creating a new system on a budget, there are a variety of other options that can be used instead of buying net pots. For example, plastic cups with lots of holes in them, or simply fine netting on a wireframe. Use your imagination!

Chapter 14

Hydroponics media

Soil-free growing mediums are primarily used in most hydroponic gardens to start seeds and for root cuttings. The lesser a hydroponic system requires, the easier it is to operate, and the less expensive it is. This is a crucial factor for commercial growers to profit from their hydroponic gardens.

An optimal medium will hold nearly the same air and water concentration. Having said earlier, to reach their roots, plants need both oxygen and nutrients. A growing medium's water/air holding capacity is determined by the small spaces between each granule or fiber. Such medium "holes" are known as "interstitial spaces." Fine sand is distinguished by tiny interstitial spaces that cannot contain much air and water. Coarse gravel has large interstitial spaces that can hold a lot of water and air. And, as nature would have it, the water runs right through it once the interstitial space becomes too wide for capillary action to keep the water in place.

The Perfect Medium:

- Holds an even air to water concentration.

- It helps shift the pH gradient.

- It is quickly flushed and re-wets after being dehydrated, as would be the case during storage.

- To ensure safe disposal, it can be reused or biodegraded.

- It's cheap and easy to get.

- It should be lightweight and user-friendly both indoors and outdoors.

Based on their origins, there are three main groups of hydroponic media: Media originating from stone or rock, Synthetics-derived media, Organic media.

Media originating from rock or stone

· Perlite

Perlite is produced from volcanic rocks heated to extreme temperatures and then erupts like popcorn, resulting in a transparent, porous medium. It's existed longer than any other hydroponic medium. Perlite has excellent oxygen retention, made of air-puffed glass pellets and almost as light as air. The main reason it is a substitute in soil and soil-free mixtures is its ability to retain oxygen. Perlite can be used loose forms, in pots, or in slim plastics sleeves, called "growing bags" because the ideal way to grow the plants is in the bags. Plants are usually installed using a drip feed system in Perlite grow bags. Perlite grow bags hold three or four long-term plants.

Perlite's most significant disadvantage is its lightweight consistency, making washing away easy. This disadvantage makes Perlite an inappropriate medium in hydroponic systems of flood and flush type or those that would be subjected to strong winds and rains if located outside.

· Rockwool

Rockwool is a molten rock derivative. It is also heated to high temperatures, but then spun into thin, insulation-like fibers. Such fibers are then compressed into cubes and slabs for hydroponic growth, or sold loose as "flocks." The cubes are widely used for plant propagation, and slabs are used similarly as perlite growing bags. On the Rockwool slab, a plant is put and grown there. The roots of the seed grow into the slab. Usually, Rockwool slabs hold three or four long-term plants. Rockwool has long been an alternative to fiberglass to building insulation and has been a pillar of commercial hydroponics for the past 20 years. It absorbs water readily and has stable drainage properties, which is why it is commonly used as a seed starting medium and also a root cutting medium.

· Lightweight Expanded Clay Aggregate (LECA)

LECA is a very coarse growing medium. Geolite, Grorox, and Hydroton are some of its common trade names. LECA consists of enlarged clay pellets, which can hold water because of their porosity and surface area.

These media are pH neutral and reusable, making them ideally suited for hydroponic systems. Although lava rocks have some of the same characteristics, they should never be used in hydroponic systems because they change the pH and leave behind a thick residue that can damage different types of equipment.

- Vermiculite

Vermiculite is a mineral that expands due to inter-laminary heat when exposed to high temperatures. It is rarely used alone; it is usually combined with other growth materials, especially Perlite. Vermiculite is an excellent medium because it allows the retention of water, moisture, and nutrients.

- Gravels

Gravel is much the same as sand, with differences in particle size only. The particles of gravel are generally 2 to 15 mm in diameter, while the particles of sand are smaller but still gritty. Sand is more likely to hold water than gravel.

- Scoria

Scoria is a porous volcanic rock that can be obtained in a wide variety of grades (i.e., diameters or sizes). Scoria's physical properties are excellent, but its pH can vary considerably depending on where it originates (pH 7 to 10). Typically, the value of scoria depends on the distance it is to be transported to. If you're close to a quarry of scoria, it can be cheap; it can be expensive if you're some distance away.

- Pumice

This is a silica volcanic rock compressed and tested before use. Its characteristics are very similar to Perlite except that it is heavier and does not so readily absorb water. To build a hydroponic base, Pumice is sometimes combined with peat and sand.

Medium derived from synthetic materials

· Sponge Foams

Sponge-like materials in some parts of the world (e.g., Florida) are

increasingly used for propagation (cutting). In hydroponic culture, the same materials were used successfully. Foams are used commercially in the Netherlands and Canada for hydroponics. Typically, they are costly.

· Expanded plastics

These materials are inert and relatively cheap in many instances. Their main disadvantages are: They do not perform well in the retention of moisture and nutrients. They are versatile, and when mixed with other materials, they often float to the top (after several months of use, what was originally a mixture will end up as a layer of expanded plastic on top of the rest of the media).

Practically no plant support is provided (trellis is vital). Such products can sometimes be beneficial when used on their own in a situation of continuous flow irrigation (automatic watering). Examples include balls of polystyrene (beanbag), Styrofoam (a mixture of ureaformaldehyde and polystyrene). Ureaformaldehyde slowly releases nitrogen through slow decomposition into solution. When used for long periods, formaldehyde residues can harm plants.

Organic media

- Sawdust

Sawdust was commonly used in industrial hydroponics in British Columbia and Canada, primarily due to its quality. Before use, hardwood sawdust (e.g., eucalyptus) should be composted. You should never use some softwood sawdust because they contain highly toxic chemicals. For short-term growth without composting (e.g., for propagation but not for growing a six-month crop), Pinus radiata sawdust succeeded. Sawdust will decompose as the crop grows if not first composted. Throughout this process, the bacteria will extract nitrogen from the nutrient solution leaving insufficient quantities for the plants • Peat moss is excavated in cold temperate climates from swampy soil. It is the remnants of plants partly decomposed (mainly mosses and sedges). The peat's basic properties can vary from deposit to deposit, although these generalizations can be made:

- Peat has a high capacity to store water.

- Sphagnum peats have better aeration when they are wet than sedge peats.

- They are not wholly nutrient-free. Some peats have much more mineral salts in them than others.

- Fully decomposed types are not appropriate for soil-free farming.

- Peat is generally acidic (sometimes as low as 4.0).

- All peats have a high capacity for pH buffering.

- They have a high capacity for cation exchange.

- When it dries out, the peat repels water. Be careful not to allow the medium's

surface to become dry. Peat is useful as a hydroponic media additive to increase cation exchange capacity, especially in run-to-waste systems. However, it will bring micronutrients to the system that could upset the nutrient solution's balance. In hydroponic cultivation, only coarse grade, high-quality peat should be used.

· Coir fiber (coconut fiber)

Coir fiber has been graciously accepted as a hydroponic growing medium of high quality and is available as a thin, granular substance in several propagation cubes, blocks, Rockwool-like slabs. When used as a growing medium, coir fines should be combined with longer fibers, while fines alone are suitable for raising seeds.

Coir has a high capacity for moisture-holding and air-filled porosity and has a long-term structure. It can be used for several years as a growing medium and sterilized between crops. Some coir supplies that may be contaminated with high sodium levels should be taken good care of. To avoid this problem, hydroponic growers should always choose' sodium-free' horticultural grade coir.

· Composted bark

The use of composted bark has become popular as a peat substitute, providing an excellent seed germination medium and hydroponic substrates. To create a stabilized product suitable for hydroponic use, bark for horticultural use is pre-composted with additional nitrogen. Often, the bark is preferable to peat if the right grade is chosen. Hydroponic bark media should consist of ground fines and coarser particles resistant to packing when in use and retain high aeration levels.

Conclusion

Hydroponics is gaining momentum and popularity rapidly, as the best way to grow everything from flowers and food to medicine. You should now be on the right track to harvest your first hydroponic crop. I hope I answered all beginning steps and gave you a solid understanding of the hydroponic process.

Having learned more about hydroponics, it is an essential type of agricultural technology as it minimizes the use of limited land space here. I believe that the future of agriculture lies with high-tech farming.

In doing so, you'll experience a revolutionary life-changing way of growing seven to ten times the amount of organic produce in the same space a soil garden takes. Gardening hydroponics puts an end to weeding and the fight against crop pests. No tilling, digging, spreading fertilizers, or shredding compost.

In this sense, I hope that I have showed you the hydroponic cultivation and explained it well to you so that everyone can benefits. But to continue with the cycle and different methods of Hydroponics by experimenting at home with indoor systems before a beginner begins a commercial hydroponic farm. At least one growth cycle of plants in hydroponics is better.

This will help you to better understand the process and the commitment of the farm from your point of view. You are going to learn from your mistakes and learn to escape certain situations. It is better to learn this stuff to a lesser degree than to cost you a lot on a business level. I wish all our readers and enthusiasts of hydroponics a good chance to start their hydroponics. I am sure about this knowledge that I have provided may help new hydroponic enthusiasts in their agriculture.

CPSIA information can be obtained
at www.ICGtesting.com
Printed in the USA
BVHW040921191120
593716BV00004B/38